Green Cuisine

for complete health

A Collection by Margaret Owens

Pacific Press®
Publishing Association

Nampa, Idaho | Oshawa, Ontario, Canada
www.pacificpress.com

Designed by Second Arrow Creative
Photography from Laurie Coates and sourced stock images

Copyright © 2018 by Pacific Press® Publishing Association
Printed in the United States of America
All rights reserved

Additional copies of this book may be purchased by calling toll-free
1-800-765-6955 or by visiting AdventistBookCenter.com.

ISBN 978-0-8163-6381-0

January 2018

"Whole-food to make you feel good"

When it comes to successfully combating the epidemic of heart disease, diabetes, excess weight, and high blood pressure, nothing in effectiveness trumps a plant-based, whole-food centered diet. This cookbook embodies these principles. You will thrive and experience health, vitality, and joy without the looming threat of chronic disease and premature death.

And you will enjoy these mouthwatering recipes.
You can do them.

Bon Appetit!

Dr. Hans Diehl

Founder of CHIP & Lifestyle Medicine Institute,

Clinical Professor of Preventive Medicine,

Loma Linda University, School of Medicine,
Loma Linda, California.

Green Cuisine for Complete Health

I love that it is prefaced with guides to clearly explain staple ingredients and spices. It's also clear that you have done due diligence with nutritional research; your recommendations are steeped in good evidence, which is super refreshing!

I can only imagine the time and effort required to compile a book like this. There is true heart on every page.

Kali Gray

APD, Dietitian & Nutritionist

B. Nutr Diet

Dedication

This book is dedicated to all those who wish to improve their health, lifestyle, and quality of life by changing to a plant-based, whole-foods centered diet.

Recipes found here will help encourage each person to continue the journey to better health.

ACKNOWLEDGMENTS:

Writing is a lonely business, but no book is produced alone. My thanks go to my husband, Peter, my toughest critic and greatest support, and my family for their wonderful encouragement.

A special mention to Dr. Hans Diehl, who read the draft manuscript and gave his valued opinion, suggestions, and comments, and to Brenda Matthews, without whom this book may not have been completed.

Contents

"Do the best you can until you know better. Then when you know better, do better." MAYA ANGELOU

About the Author

Margaret Owens—BSN, GrDip Adult Education and Tertiary

Living in the country in New Zealand, I had an ideal childhood. We had our own jersey dairy cow, hens, chickens, and pet sheep—plus a dog and cats. This means we had all the milk, cream, and eggs we wanted. Oatmeal porridge was cooked for breakfast most mornings with a generous serving of milk or cream. However, as my father was Scottish, he allowed us only a little salt and sweetening of any kind on our cereal was "out." Meat or fish was provided at Christmas only, which was a special time when sweets, as a rare treat, were allowed in our Christmas stockings.

On the other hand, we were fortunate to have nearly all the fresh vegetables we needed for a family of six in that our mother maintained a productive vegetable garden. Even fresh field mushrooms were harvested from the fields in autumn and walnuts were picked from our walnut tree. While we as children longed to experience the city life, our city cousins, on the other hand, delighted in staying with us in the country whenever they could.

After leaving home to commence my nursing training, meals were provided for us. Looking back, I now realize that hospital food may not be the closest to an ideal and healthy diet. Even so, being away from home meant a newfound level of independence and freedom. And I exercised it: I added meat to my basically lacto-ovo vegetarian diet and I enjoyed it.

Over the years, I furthered my nursing career, gained a few extra certificates, and found myself in the cardiology specialty, and—loving it! Working with highly motivated nursing staff and with experienced and dynamic cardiologists, it was obvious to me: I had found my niche. How I enjoyed spending time with my patients, instructing them how to improve their lifestyle, how to get into an exercise program, and how to make wiser dietary choices. Little did I understand, however, that offering advice and education during the acute phase of an illness when many patients find themselves often in a state of denial and not feeling well at all, was probably not the best time for them to absorb my well-intended instruction.

Over time, I noticed that some patients were admitted several times with the same symptoms. For them, the hospital became a revolving door. And yet each time, we rushed to their rescue. We used the latest diagnostic techniques, the newest breakthrough medications, and the most advanced surgical procedures, all designed to save lives and to make the patient feel comfortable—largely treating the symptoms of an underlying devastating disease called atherosclerosis. This circulation-affecting disease, characterized by inflammation and a narrowing and hardening of the arteries, we rarely touched with our high-tech approach. And so it progressed unaltered until the next crisis emerged, expressing itself as coronary artery disease, myocardial infarction, angina pectoris, stroke, hypertension, hearing and vision loss, cognitive diminishment, erectile dysfunction . . . largely chronic conditions.

What I have learned over the years is that many of these circulation related diseases are largely lifestyle related and can be reversed. I have seen inspiring clinical results and disease turnarounds, as patients and people attending community based education programs embrace a simpler diet and often within weeks see their high levels of blood sugar, blood pressure, and cholesterol drop so low that their physicians had to reduce and often discontinue their medications. At the same time, their angina pain diminished, their sleep apnoea often became just a memory, and they rejoiced in losing weight while eating more, but of the right foods.

This book is a small contribution to help people make and sustain wiser dietary choices.

Introduction

More and more people are being drawn to a more plant-based, whole-food centered diet. Some adopt a more "foods-as-grown" diet for health reasons, others do it for ethical, ecological, or spiritual reasons. Whatever their reason for choosing this natural foods option, their decision opens a door into an exciting culinary world of creativity and substantial health benefits in the short and long term.

My reasons for choosing this option relate to the benefits in health, ethics, ecology, and spirituality. There is no doubt that a plant-based, whole-foods centered diet is the healthiest way to eat. The evidence is overwhelming: scientific and medical research strongly supports this view. In regards to the environmental concerns, John McDougall, MD, a best-selling medical and health author, cited a major report from the World Health Organization that raising livestock (cows, pigs, chickens, etc.) to feed people produces more greenhouse gases than all the transportation (cars, trains, airplanes, etc.) in the world combined. Quite alarming, the estimated greenhouse gas contribution from people eating meat, poultry, dairy, and eggs since 2006 has risen more than 50 percent. As for ethical considerations, my concerns are for the welfare of animals in these awful factory farms where they hardly see the light of day and are caged to restrict movement for greater profits.

Many of our modern diseases, such as heart disease, stroke, diabetes, hypertension, obesity, diverticulitis, and some adult cancers are directly related to a diet high in fat, sugar, and salt and low in nutritional density and fiber. Changing to foods-as-grown, such as whole grains, legumes, fruits, and vegetables and limiting processed and animal foods would powerfully reduce the incidence of modern chronic diseases and facilitate their arrest and reversal.

My background in cardiac nursing helped me to better understand that our current medical model will often at best provide symptomatic relief without offering an effective cure. Later, when I came across the Complete Health Improvement Program (CHIP), an intensive educational lifestyle intervention program modeled after the new lifestyle medicine concept, I recognized the benefits of using this health program to help prevent, arrest, and even reverse many of our modern killer diseases. Totally evidence based, CHIP stresses the need for people to become informed with the wealth of scientific information so that they can make more intelligent choices and wisely assume more responsibility for their own health. After all, no one should care for their health more than we as a people.

This book aims to make it easier for the readers to choose healthier and more environmentally friendly culinary options and to share them with others. With a table attractively arranged, and the food garnished and pleasingly presented, it has been my experience that many will not even notice the absence of animal products.

In this book I have tried to open a small door into this wider culinary world by introducing a few of those ingredients that are not generally used in our home kitchens but can be found in some gourmet recipe books, selective food stores, and markets.

Where did I obtain these recipes? I have gathered some from friends and family members, others from toying with recipes on the backs of packets and magazines, and yet others are the result of trying dishes that have impressed me at various restaurants I have visited. I have taken the ideas home and experimented in my kitchen until I achieved a similar result.

Nothing would give me more pleasure than to hear from you about your journey into a new world of taste and better health.

How to Use these Recipes

When preparing food, fill your plate with vegetables, whole grains, legumes, and fruit. And where possible, offer them in either their raw state or lightly cooked. Aim to purchase the freshest fruit and vegetables. These are often found in those smaller grocery stores or local produce markets. Zero in on produce in season. When you do this, you avoid items that have lost some of their food value due to cold storage and lengthy transportation times. Planting and harvesting one's own vegetables even in small home gardens is most rewarding and ensures the freshest of produce.

Many of my recipes in this book have quantities sufficient for four people. I have found that most people wishing to make healthier dietary choices are either couples or single people. With that in mind, it is easier for them to halve the quantities given here, so they are not left with a large amount to store. On the other hand, why not cook larger amounts and freeze leftovers for future use? For those of you who have a wheat intolerance, I have identified recipes that are gluten free with "GF."

Many recipes that usually employ meat, fish, or chicken can easily be replaced with tofu, herbs, and spices or by simply adding more vegetables and legumes. Since a reduction in fat, sugar, and salt in our dishes removes much of the "artificial" flavor, it is essential to replace them with ingredients such as herbs and those spices that are found particularly in Middle Eastern, Mediterranean, and Asian cuisine. As you begin to feel more confident in your new and exciting culinary journey, you may want to experiment with new tastes and flavors outside the ones mentioned in this book.

For many Asian vegetarian dishes, chefs will replace fish and oyster sauces with a low salt soy sauce for color diluted with water along with the scant use of other ingredients such as rice vinegar and sugar or pineapple juice to create a delicately flavored sauce. On the other hand, you can also simply replace these ingredients with a low salt soy sauce, such as tamari, which is suitable for those with gluten intolerance.

THE FRESHEST FRUIT AND VEGETABLES ARE OFTEN FOUND IN SMALLER GROCERY STORES OR LOCAL PRODUCE MARKETS WHEN IN SEASON.

Tips For Cooking

Eggs are not used in this book. My reasons are: about 70 percent of calories in an egg are from fat, a large proportion of that is saturated fat. The yolk is loaded with cholesterol (about 213 mg per egg) while the white is high in animal protein. Because their shells are fragile and porous and conditions on egg farms are crowded, eggs are the perfect host for salmonella—the bacteria responsible for many food poisoning cases. It is easy to substitute eggs in a recipe. The main function of eggs in baking is to bind the other ingredients together and to help lighten the texture.

HERE ARE THREE SUGGESTED SUBSTITUTES FOR EGGS IN BAKING:

1. Apple sauce: Three Tbsp of apple sauce is equivalent to one egg.
2. Potato starch: One Tbsp of potato starch or cornstarch and 3 Tbsp of water is equivalent to one egg.
3. Bananas: While they may leave a slight banana flavor to the cooked product, they help bind the ingredients in place of egg. Half a mashed banana is equivalent to one egg.

COOKING DRIED BEANS AND PEAS

Be sure you rinse them well and drain them after soaking. Cooking time can vary depending on the cooking method and the type of bean used. Here are three methods that I recommend.

1. Pressure cooker method:

Pick over dried beans or peas and wash and drain them a couple of times. Then soak them for 8 hours. Drain and rinse them once more. Place beans/peas in a pressure cooker with, 1–2 bay leaves, 1 onion studded with 8–10 whole cloves, and a Tbsp of oil. Follow manufacturer's instructions regarding the amount of water to be added and the recommended cooking times. The addition of oil is to prevent excessive frothing when cooking.

2. Boiling method:

Pick beans/peas over and wash and drain them a couple of times. Soak them in plenty of water for about 8 hours. Drain and rinse them once more. Add them to boiling water (2 cups beans to 6 cups of water) with an onion studded with cloves, a bay leaf, and a Tbsp of oil.

Cook for 2–4 hours until soft. If you use salt, then always add it at the end of the cooking time.

3. Deep freeze method:

Dried beans and peas can be stored, after soaking, draining, and drying, in an airtight container in the freezer for several weeks. When taken out they are then ready for grinding for use in patties, etc.

NOTE: All recipes have been tried and tested. The flavors in a recipe, however, that appeal to one may not necessarily appeal to another. Therefore, experiment with those flavors that you prefer.

USEFUL ITEMS FOR YOUR KITCHEN

Slow Cooker

Pressure Cooker

Coffee Grinder for Spices

Heavy Based Saucepan

Healthy Ingredients

legumes

Legumes are usually classified as peas, beans, and lentils. Among them are soy beans, pinto beans, lima beans, red beans, black eyed peas, chickpeas (or garbanzo beans), dhal, moong, and many more. They are, nutritionally speaking, a royal food, high in fiber and an excellent source of protein, potassium, iron, some of the B group of vitamins, and some trace elements such as manganese and copper. There are over 40 types of beans and peas. Many of them can be sprouted and turned into bean sprouts. Legumes are an outstanding source of protein. The Asian world has depended on these foods for thousands of years. It is here that the full range of bean dishes from appetizers to snacks has been thoroughly explored.

buckwheat

While many people think of buckwheat as a cereal grain, it is actually a fruit seed that is related to rhubarb and sorrel. This makes buckwheat grain a substitute for people who are wheat and gluten sensitive. It is a rich source of fiber, protein, and iron.

agar-agar

Agar-agar is a jelly-like substance obtained from algae. It is derived from the polysaccharide agarose, which forms the supporting structure in the cell walls of certain species of algae. Those who prefer not to use animal products can use it as a substitute for any dish that recommends gelatin. It is generally found in Asian supermarkets and health food stores. It has no taste, odor, or color and sets more firmly than gelatin, even at room temperature.

To prepare agar-agar, place 200 mls water into a small pan or pot, then gradually add the agar-agar whisking until completely dissolved. Bring agar-agar to a simmer and continue to gently cook for 5–6 mins while stirring. It sets as it cools. It is recommended to have both the mixture and agar-agar at about the same temperature when adding agar. If mixture is too cool, the agar will form clumps when added.

soy sauce

Soy sauce and its many forms are found widely throughout Asia. Tamari, a Japanese form of soy sauce, is traditionally made as a by-product of miso paste. For those who are gluten intolerant, use tamari. Otherwise use one of the low salt soy sauces. It is often used in Asian cuisine to replace fish and oyster sauces.

tofu

Tofu, also known as bean curd, is a food made by coagulating soy milk and then pressing the resulting curds into soft white blocks. Tofu is most versatile and a much used ingredient in Asian cuisines. It is a great substitute for meat, fish, and seafood. Tofu comes in various forms: soft, firm, marinated, or fried. It can also be deep frozen.

lentils

A small but nutritionally mighty member of the legume family. Lentils are a very good source of fiber. They are therapeutically ideal in managing diabetic blood sugar levels in that their high fiber content prevents blood sugar levels from rising rapidly after a meal. Lentils are a good source of many minerals, fiber, B-vitamins, and protein, while at the same time very low in fat.

dried fruit	Dried fruits are known for their alkalinity, but use them in judicious amounts since they are high in calories (fructose) due to their concentrated form. In addition, some imported fruits, such as dates and apricots, are usually treated with sulphur dioxide. If you are concerned about this, boil the fruit for one minute, and then discard the water. Otherwise, buy the local country's produce.
rolled oats	Oats are a low acid and low glycemic index (GI) food. Rolled oats are usually steamed or toasted and then rolled. Oats are fragmented to different degrees; a more fragmented product will cook more quickly as it absorbs water more readily. The amount of bran retained in rolled oats also varies. It may be better to use Scottish oats, whole-grain oats, or oat groats where more of the outer bran layer is retained. This food is low in sodium, and is a good source of protein, dietary fiber, thiamine, magnesium, and phosphorus, and a very good source of manganese.
besan flour	Also known as chickpea or gram flour, besan flour is higher in dietary fiber and plant protein than the common wheat flour. It is also rich in various nutrients such as iron, zinc, and potassium. Used widely in Indian cuisine, it can be used in place of wheat flour for those with gluten intolerance.
grains	Grains or cereals are probably the most widely used staple food of all. They are high in fiber, iron, magnesium, selenium (necessary in the maintenance of a healthy immune system), and several of the B group of vitamins. Wheat, rye, oats, millet, barley, maize, and rice are the main food groups and are of most benefit when purchased in the unprocessed form.
nuts and seeds	Nuts and seeds are nutritious and are recommended for daily use. They are high in plant proteins and many of the B group vitamins and minerals yet, because of their high fat and calorie content, they should be eaten only in moderation.
seaweed	As dark, leafy vegetables go, seaweed is about as nutrient-dense as it gets. Eat about a gram of seaweed and your daily iodine needs are taken care of. Seaweed packs super-high amounts of calcium—higher than broccoli—and in terms of protein, it's almost as rich as legumes. There's also a good number of vitamins A and B_{12} and it's a great source of soluble fiber. It is an ideal ingredient when preparing vegetable stocks.
oils	Because of their very high caloric density and their contribution to excess weight, the use of all fats and oils are restricted. Vegetable oils when hydrogenated through high temperature processes create dangerous trans fats that directly contribute to coronary heart disease. They are so health erosive, that they are no longer allowed to be used in the US. Saturated fats, commonly found in meats, sausages, and dairy but also in palm and coconut oil, are the number one driver of high blood and cholesterol levels, that in turn drive the heart disease epidemic.

Spices & Other Flavors

caperberries and capers	Not generally interchangeable, though they both derive from the same plant, which grows throughout the Mediterranean. The round, lemony, small capers are not the berries. These tiny pea-like bursts of flavor are actually immature buds of the caper bush. In addition to the tiny buds, caperberries are also harvested and some may prefer their taste to the stronger caper buds. Though they still have some lemony taste, they are much milder than caper buds. Generally, when a recipe calls for caperberries, using capers instead will provide too much acid in a dish.
chia seeds	The highest plant-based source of dietary fiber, protein and antioxidants, they are full of nature's perfectly balanced omega 3–6-9s, fiber, and vitamins A, C, and minerals such as calcium, iron, and magnesium. Chia is a staple food of Mexico, Peru, Chile, and Bolivia. It is also gluten free.
guar gum	A stabilizer and thickening agent and is suitable for those with gluten intolerance when it is made from rye, barley, or oats. Simply ensure when purchasing that its origin is not wheat. Unlike agar-agar, it does not have to be heated to begin activation. Guar gum is a protein found in wheat, oats, rye, and barley and can be bought in most health food stores and some supermarkets.
kombu	A calcium-rich dried kelp, used in making stock and preserves, Kombu can be purchased from most Asian stores, some health-food stores, and selective supermarkets. Wipe the leaf lightly with a damp cloth if a light dusting of powdery substance is present so as not to remove the flavor that is near the surface. Store kombu in an airtight container in the refrigerator.
miso paste	A blend of salt, soy beans, and either rice or barley, which is fermented and ground. The end result is a unique condiment that contains protein, dietary fiber and iron. Miso comes in a variety of types and colors but in this book we use the white miso (sometimes yellow), which is relatively sweet and is mainly used in soups, stews, sauces, and vegetable dishes. It can be purchased from Asian stores and selective supermarkets.
orange flower water	A natural extract made from the distillation of orange blossoms. Orange flower water is used in Middle Eastern cooking in both savory and sweet foods. The price is normally an indication of quality.

quinoa	Pronounced *keen-wa*, it originated in South America, where it has been grown for hundreds of years. It is not a true grain but is a seed from the goosefoot plant that is used as a grain. Quinoa seed is high in protein, calcium, and iron and is a relatively good source of vitamin E and several of the B group of vitamins. While low in sodium, quinoa provides valuable starch and fiber. The seeds should be refrigerated; their shelf life is 12 months.
rosewater	A classic Persian ingredient with a history dating back to ancient times. It is a lavish addition to desserts and some savory dishes. It has a very delicate flavor, so if you haven't used it before, try using it here.
saffron	The world's most expensive spice and is derived from the stigmas of the purple saffron crocus. Only very small quantities are required to add color and aroma to a dish. To obtain maximum flavor, dry-roast it first over low heat. Stir until threads turn dark reddish brown. Crumble threads into a small amount of hot dairy-free milk. Allow saffron to soak for a couple of hours and then add to your dish.
textured vegetable protein (tvp)	Also known as textured soy protein (tsp), it can come as soya meat, soya chunks, and soya mince amongst others. It is a by-product of extracting soybean oil. It is often used as a meat enhancer or replacement. It is quick to cook and has a protein content far greater than that of meat.
verjus	The unfermented juice of premium wine grapes, verjus adds a gentle acidity and a lovely piquancy to almost any food and is milder than lemon. If verjus is not available, exchange it for non-alcoholic white wine or lemon juice. Verjus should be available in most good stores or supermarkets. If not, ask the manager if they can procure it for you.
tamarind paste	Is prepared from tamarind—a sticky sour tasting fruit that grows on bean-like pods on tamarind trees. It is a must have ingredient in most, if not all, Thai recipes especially in savory dishes. It can be purchased in Asian and Indian food stores.
cinnamon	It is better to use Ceylon ("true" cinnamon). The Cassia variety contains significant amounts of a compound called coumarin, which is believed to be harmful in large doses. Unfortunately, most cinnamon found in supermarkets is the cheaper Cassia variety. Try substituting cinnamon requirements by preparing 1 part coriander seed and 1 part sweet anise seed. Grind in a coffee mill. Store in a labeled container in a cool dry place.

galangal	Galangal is a member of the ginger family, also known as Laos root. It has a woody texture and is used to give flavor to Thai and other South East Asian cuisines.
sumac	Sumac spice is extracted from the berries of a bush that grows wild in the Mediterranean region and ground into a deep maroon colored powder. This spice is used in Middle Eastern cooking to add a tangy, citrus, lemony flavor with a sweet note to dishes.
garam masala	This spice is a crucial mix in many Indian recipes. You can buy it premade, but it's infinitely better to make your own, which is fresher than the bought variety. Garam masala is best when made with whole spices that are roasted and ground at home.
turmeric	Turmeric has a peppery, warm, and bitter flavor with a mild fragrance slightly reminiscent of orange and ginger. It is best known as one of the ingredients used to make curry. Turmeric is an old Indian spice with a powerful medicinal compound called curcumin.
cardamom	Cardamom is the world's third-most expensive spice by weight, outstripped in market value only by saffron and vanilla, but little is needed to impart flavor. It is best stored in pod form because once the seeds are exposed or ground, they quickly lose their flavor. When cardamom is stored in an airtight (preferably a vacuum) container at temperatures below the freezing point of water, it can retain its flavor for many years. It is a commonly used ingredient in Indian cooking.
sweet paprika	Fresh paprika has a full, sweet pepper flavor without the heat. It's not just a pretty garnishing color! This very high quality paprika from the Kalocsa region of Hungary bears the name Csemege, or "exquisite delicacy." It has a reputation as the most flavorful of all paprikas.
himalayan salt	Himalayan salt is the purest organic salt on this planet and contains 84 minerals and trace elements essential for the human body's growth and well-being. One tsp salt per day is all that is necessary for body requirements.
cayenne pepper	Cayenne pepper is great to add another dimension to a dish—just a little sprinkle may not actually add much heat, but can enhance the other flavors. The spice contains very high levels of essential minerals. When consumed in small quantities regularly, cayenne provides sufficient levels of iron, copper, zinc, potassium, manganese, magnesium, and selenium.

CAYENNE PEPPER CONTAINS HIGH LEVELS OF MANY ESSENTIAL MINERALS.

"Getting healthy can give you a longer happier life." DR. H. DIEHL, DHSc

To Start the Day

Have you heard the saying, "Eat like a king for breakfast, a prince for lunch, and a pauper for tea"? If we were all prepared to take this advice, fewer of us would suffer from obesity as a good breakfast reduces the desire to "graze" through the day when many extra calories are consumed. With a lighter evening meal, we would also probably sleep better at night.

A wholesome breakfast provides the nutritional and colonic foundation for the day. With a bit of effort, it can be prepared before retiring at night so that it is waiting, cooked for you in the morning. It has been shown to improve a child's attention span, reduce aggressiveness in the school playground, and increase the child's ability to learn. But avoid processed breakfast cereals that are high in salt and sugar, and poor in fiber and nutritional content.

SELECT CEREALS HIGH IN FIBER AND NUTRITIONAL CONTENT.

"The fat you eat is the fat you wear."

J. MCDOUGALL, MD

pistachio, cranberry & apricot quinoa porridge, p. 19

FIVE GRAINS FOR CEREAL

whole wheat rolled or flaked

whole rye rolled or flaked

whole barley rolled or flaked

brown rice flaked

whole rolled oats

amaranth seed (use whole)

quinoa (use whole)

1 cup of 5 grain cereal

3–3 ½ cups water

½ tsp salt

4 fresh dates, chopped

1 red apple, grated

½ cup sultanas (raisins)

SERVES 4

This cereal is an excellent source of fiber and makes a most satisfying breakfast dish.

It is preferable to purchase these grains in either rolled or flake form as they are easier to cook. In addition, they are more palatable. If you cannot find them in rolled or flaked form, then try pulse blending them in a good strong blender for around 3 seconds to break those grains a little. Refrigerate left-over quantities in a sealed container for future use.

Use equal quantities of 5 of the listed grains for 5 grain cereal. If you have access to other grains, then use them as well.

FIVE GRAIN CEREAL

Jean Gidley Ward

Place all ingredients in a slow cooker and stir well. Soak for 6–8 hrs then turn the setting to high and cook for 4 hrs. Use a timer, if you intend to cook the cereal through the night.

TIP: If you require gluten free, replace whole wheat with quinoa or amaranth seed that are available in good supermarkets or health food stores.

Here is my recommendation: Soak for 6–8 hrs and then cook for 4 hrs. Try preparing the evening prior, using a 3–4 quart slow cooker and a timer set to start around 2:00 a.m. so that by 6:00 a.m. it is cooked and ready to serve. Those commencing work early have a hot substantial start for the day. This long slow process allows for the fiber to be well soaked and completely cooked, limiting for some the uncomfortable effects of a high fiber meal. I recommend 1 part cereal to 3½ parts of water for a softer consistency. For a firmer consistency add less water.

PER SERVING	Calories 89	Protein 2g	Fat 1g	Carbohydrates 18g	Sugar 16g	Fiber 3g	Sodium 289mg

BAKED OATMEAL GF

Linda Owens

This breakfast dish was first introduced to me by our daughter-in-law. I enjoyed it so much that she gave me the recipe. Here it is:

Preheat oven to 350°F. Reserve 1 Tbsp each of the berries, nuts, and dates for garnishing later.

Mix the rest of the ingredients in a large bowl and spoon into a casserole dish. Place into preheated oven and bake for around 45 mins. Garnish surface with the remaining fruit and nuts before serving.

2 cups oatmeal

1 cup barley

4½ cups warm water

2 Tbsp chia seeds

3 tsp honey

¼ cup quinoa flakes

2 Tbsp shredded coconut

pinch of salt

1 cup frozen mixed berries

½ cup mixed nuts (chopped), dates and/or dried fruit of your choice

SERVES 4

PER SERVING	Calories 310	Protein 9g	Fat 9g	Carbohydrates 48g	Sugar 9g	Fiber 10g	Sodium 103mg

BEST SERVED WITH WARM NONDAIRY MILK

PISTACHIO, CRANBERRY & APRICOT QUINOA PORRIDGE GF

2 cups quinoa (see p. 10)

5 cups water

½ cup nondairy milk

¼ cup dried apricots, chopped

¼ cup dried cranberries

¼ cup pistachio nuts, chopped

SERVES 4

First tried at a restaurant, I enjoyed it so much that I now serve it on occasions for breakfast at our home.

Gently cook quinoa in the water over a gentle heat in a covered saucepan for 25–30 mins or until quinoa is light, fluffy, and soft to taste. Add ¾ of the apricots, cranberries, and nuts (reserving the remainder for the garnish) while cooking quinoa. Add enough milk to keep quinoa moist.

Serve in warm bowls and top with the rest of the dried fruit and nuts. Top with a drizzle of honey if desired.

PER SERVING	Calories 417	Protein 15g	Fat 8g	Carbohydrates 69g	Sugar 20g	Fiber 9g	Sodium 296mg

CHIA SEED PORRIDGE GF

½ cup chia seeds (see p. 9)

3–3½ cups of water or nondairy milk (or a combination of both)

2 tsp honey

½ tsp salt

4 strawberries

2 tsp toasted slivered or flaked almonds (optional)

SERVES 4

I first tried this porridge in a local restaurant. I liked it so much that I experimented at home until I thought this dish was similar in taste and texture. And here it is! Despite the relatively high fat content of chia seeds, I have included it as it is a valuable and nutritious food source. As an option try adding a few Tbsp of coconut milk to add some creaminess.

Place chia seeds in a large bowl and gradually add the liquid while whisking continuously to prevent seeds from clumping, until all the milk/water has been added.

Cover and refrigerate overnight. In the morning check consistency and add more milk or water if desired.

Heat chia seeds in a saucepan or microwave and serve when well warmed through.

Add a small drizzle of honey to each plate. Garnish with a fanned strawberry or a few flaked or slivered almonds.

PER SERVING	Calories 100	Protein 4g	Fat 7g	Carbohydrates 5g	Sugar 4g	Fiber 8g	Sodium 284mg

TOASTED MUESLI

Jean Gidley Ward

This is my favorite muesli recipe.

Mix all the dry ingredients in a large bowl.

Place soaked dates, water, and bananas in a blender and blend till smooth. Add to dry ingredients and mix in well.

Spread mixture on baking sheets and bake at 260°F for 1 hr 15 mins until toasted and dry. Turn muesli every 20–30 mins.

If the ingredients are still not dry, return them to the oven for another 10–15 mins until they are completely dry and crunchy. Take care not to overcook or burn the muesli.

Store muesli at room temperature in an airtight container. 1 cup per serving.

8 cups oat flakes

1 cup desiccated coconut

1 cup sunflower seeds

1 cup pepitas (pumpkin seeds)

1 cup pecan nuts

1½ cups dates, pitted (soaked in hot water for 30 mins)

2 bananas

SERVES 12

PER SERVING	Calories 500	Protein 14g	Fat 24g	Carbohydrates 57g	Sugar 19g	Fiber 12g	Sodium 7mg

BROWN RICE CEREAL GF

Start the day right! This can be cooked in advance and heated before serving. Here is my labor-saving tip: Cook enough breakfast cereal to last a couple of days and store it refrigerated.

Place brown rice and quinoa plus 3 cups water (from the 5¼ cups) in a saucepan or pot and simmer for about 20 mins.

Then add the ground flax seeds, porridge oats, and all other ingredients plus the rest of the water to the saucepan or pot.

Bring to the boil and simmer for 25 mins or until mixture is well cooked and thickened. Stir occasionally to prevent grains sticking to the base of the saucepan.

Add more water as needed to obtain desired consistency. Serve warm with a nondairy milk.

¾ cup brown rice

1 cup rolled oats

¼ cup quinoa

2 tsp flax seeds, ground

1 Tbsp sunflower seeds

1 Tbsp pepita seeds (pumpkin seeds)

4 dates, chopped

1 Tbsp sesame seeds

¼ cup sultanas (raisins)

5¼ cups water

½ tsp salt

SERVES 4

PER SERVING	Calories 320	Protein 9g	Fat 7g	Carbohydrates 55g	Sugar 7g	Fiber 5g	Sodium 276mg

BAKED BEANS 🇬🇫

1 large onion, chopped

3 cloves garlic, crushed

2 Tbsp tomato paste

30 oz chopped fresh peeled tomatoes (or 2×15 oz cans tomatoes)

7 oz dried haricot beans

2 oz dried lima beans

3.5 oz dried black eyed beans

1¼ cups water with 1 tsp stock powder (see p. 83)

2 tsp Dijon mustard

3 Tbsp tamari

1 tsp brown sugar

1 Tbsp cornstarch

SERVES 8

I serve this dish on toast. It is especially good for breakfast. I first tasted this at a local restaurant. After some experimentation in my kitchen, this emerged. I think you will enjoy this most satisfying dish as much as we do. Try making this quantity and use it for several servings. It is also nice as a filling with baked potatoes.

See p. 9 for instructions on cooking beans.

Meanwhile sauté onions and garlic (without oil), until translucent and golden, adding 2 Tbsp water if necessary to prevent burning while stirring constantly.

Next add tomato paste, chopped tomatoes, cooked beans, stock, and mustard. Stir in well.

Bring to heat and simmer gently for 20 mins to blend flavors and ingredients. Add tamari and sugar after 10 mins, again stirring well.

Stir in cornstarch mixed with ¼ cup cold water and continue stirring until mixture thickens slightly. Remove from heat and serve immediately.

Will keep refrigerated for up to a week.

PER SERVING	Calories 163	Protein 17g	Fat 3g	Carbohydrates 18g	Sugar 6g	Fiber 9g	Sodium 370mg

BEANS ARE NUTRITIONALLY AN EXCELLENT SOURCE OF PROTEIN AND FIBER.

Lite Bites

Lite Bites are interesting, tasty, light morsels served either prior to the main meal or on the arrival of guests and served with liquid refreshments. Here are some dips that I have included for your enjoyment.

SERVE WITH
FRESHLY BAKED
LEBANESE CRISPS
(P. 82)

"Take a drink of water. It passes right through, giving everything a good rinse." A. LUDINGTON, MD, AND DR. H. DIEHL, DHSc

HUMMUS GF

1–2 cloves garlic, peeled

½ small onion, chopped

2 Tbsp tahini

11 oz chickpeas, cooked or canned, (rinsed and drained)

4 Tbsp lemon juice

¼ tsp salt

3–4 Tbsp water

1 tsp olive oil

¼ tsp sweet paprika or sumac

SERVES 6

I find adding a small amount of onion adds a nice bite to this dip.

Place all the ingredients (except paprika or sumac) in a food processor and blend until very smooth. For a thinner consistency add a little more cold water. Place hummus in a serving bowl and finally sprinkle with sweet paprika or sumac and refrigerate until ready to serve.

Serve with Lebanese Crisps (p. 82), crackers, or crudités. Hummus may also be added to baked potatoes in place of butter or sour cream. Keeps refrigerated for up to a week.

Makes about 2½ cups.

PER SERVING	Calories 93	Protein 5g	Fat 5g	Carbohydrates 7g	Sugar 1g	Fiber 4g	Sodium 298mg

GUACAMOLE GF

1 clove garlic

1 small onion, very finely chopped

1 small red chile, deseeded and finely chopped (optional)

2 large avocados

2 Tbsp lemon juice

¼ tsp salt

1 small tomato, skin removed, deseeded and chopped

1 pinch freshly ground black peppercorns

¼ cup fresh coriander leaves, finely chopped

SERVES 6

This is my version of a well known and much used dip. While the use of tomato in this dish is a tasty addition, it tends to color the dish a slightly mustard color. If you wish to serve a bright green guacamole leave the tomato out and avoid using over-ripe avocados.

Place the garlic, onion, and chile in a mortar and pestle and pound until a smooth paste is formed. Then place in blender with peeled avocados, lemon juice, tomato, and seasoning. Blend well. Stir in coriander, and place mixture in a serving bowl.

Cover surface of guacamole with cling wrap to prevent mixture from discoloring and refrigerate until ready to serve.

Makes 1½ cups

TIP: Guacamole may be served with crusty bread, crackers, or Lebanese Crisps (p. 82).

PER SERVING	Calories 125	Protein 2g	Fat 11g	Carbohydrates 2g	Sugar 2g	Fiber 2g	Sodium 99mg

PUMPKIN AND CUMIN DIP

This is a lovely sweet and spicy dip. A favorite of many.

Place pumpkin on a baking tray lined with parchment paper and roast (with skin) at 380°F for about 40 mins or until flesh is soft and cooked through. Allow to cool slightly before removing the flesh.

Place flesh in a food processor or bowl with ground cumin, salt, peanut butter, and chile powder. Blend thoroughly (otherwise mash well if using a bowl). Add 1–2 Tbsp water to obtain a softer consistency if desired. Spoon dip into a serving dish, sprinkle peanuts over the top, and finish with a drizzle of oil.

Refrigerate until ready to serve. Serve with savory crackers or Lebanese Crisps (p. 82). Makes about 2 cups.

1 lb pumpkin, cut into cubes

1 tsp ground cumin seeds

½ tsp salt

1 Tbsp crunchy peanut butter

½ tsp chile powder

1–2 tsp olive oil

2 Tbsp roasted peanuts, finely chopped

SERVES 6

PER SERVING	Calories 89	Protein 5g	Fat 5g	Carbohydrates 7g	Sugar 5g	Fiber 2g	Sodium 189mg

BABA GHANOUSH (CREAMED EGGPLANT WITH TAHINI)

Since I like eggplants (aubergines) I use this recipe quite often. For that extra zing I also add ½ a small chopped onion.

Preheat oven to 350°F. Wash the eggplant and prick the skin 2–3 times with a fork. Place onto baking dish or tray lined with parchment paper then place into the heated oven for ¾ to 1 hr until soft to touch.

Remove from oven, allow to cool before peeling away the skin leaving the cooked "flesh." In a blender or food processor combine the eggplant, garlic, and onion until blended. Then add all other ingredients (except the pomegranate seeds) until well combined.

Garnish with chopped parsley and pomegranate seeds. This dip may be prepared ahead of time and refrigerated for at least a day. Serve chilled accompanied with pita bread, crackers, or Lebanese Crisps (p. 82).

Makes about 2 cups.

TIP: Take care when removing pomegranate seeds: wear an apron since the seeds stain. Cut pomegranate in half, place cut-side down and firmly tap with the flat blade of a large knife. This removes the seeds. Their color is a wonderful contrast.

1 medium-sized eggplant (about 16 oz)

2 cloves garlic, peeled

½ small onion, chopped

1 Tbsp tahini

3–4 Tbsp lemon juice

¼ tsp salt

1 tsp fresh parsley, chopped

1 Tbsp pomegranate seeds (optional)

SERVES 8

PER SERVING	Calories 60	Protein 3g	Fat 4g	Carbohydrates 3g	Sugar 3g	Fiber 3g	Sodium 98mg

Antipasto is great fun and allows the chef the chance to be creative with ingredients and dressings. Here are a few suggestions. Remember you are only limited by your own imagination when putting this dish together. It looks wonderful when served creatively on a large platter.

"A WORLD WITHOUT TOMATOES IS LIKE A STRING QUARTET WITHOUT VIOLINS."
LAURIE COLWIN

ANTIPASTO (GF)

EGGPLANT

Cut lengthwise into thin strips, no need to "sweat" the vegetable if they are young and fresh. Rub both surfaces with a halved garlic clove and cook on a hot grilling plate until lightly charred. Otherwise place slices under a hot grill until slightly charred. Cool and sprinkle with balsamic vinegar. Roll into curls or place less formally on serving plate. As an alternative: eggplant slices may be rolled in sesame seeds before placing onto the serving plate.

CHICKPEAS

Mix well and allow to stand for 1 hr.

ROASTED PEPPERS

Use red or yellow. Cut peppers in half and remove seeds. Roast under a hot grill or on top of a gas flame until skin is blistered and black. Allow to cool by putting them into a bowl and cover with plastic wrap or a plate. When cool, remove skins and cut into chunks (or slice into thin strips for final garnish). To serve add a few rinsed and chopped capers, chopped oregano, and two cloves of crushed garlic.

TOMATOES

Cut tops from tomatoes and carefully scoop out seeds. Drain tomatoes upside down on absorbent paper for 30 mins. Combine hummus and parsley, mixing well. Spoon mixture carefully back into tomatoes.

As an alternative, try stuffing tomatoes with basil pesto (p. 87). They also look impressive if served on their own with a sprig of basil on the side.

ZUCCHINI

Use the blade of a potato peeler or a mandolin to make very thin slices (cut lengthwise). Blanch slices in boiling salted water for 1 minute then refresh in iced water and drain. Dress with finely chopped toasted walnuts, parsley, and a vinaigrette with a few drops of walnut oil added. Let stand for 1 hr and roll into curls before serving.

CURRIED MUSHROOMS

Remove stems from mushrooms. Place them stem side up on oven tray and grill until mushrooms begin to soften. Heat the oil in small pan and add curry powder and nuts, stirring until nuts are lightly browned. Cool. Top mushrooms with curried nuts.

BAKED GARLIC

Cut the top ¼ off the heads of garlic and discard. Place garlic in a baking dish into a preheated oven at 350°F for 45–50 mins or until soft. Individual cloves can then be easily squeezed out of their casings.

EGGPLANT

4 long thin purple eggplants

1 clove garlic

1 Tbsp balsamic vinegar

CHICKPEAS

15 oz can of chickpeas, drained and rinsed

1 small red onion, thinly sliced

grated rind of 1 small lemon

your favorite vinaigrette with lemon juice added

1 Tbsp parsley, chopped (or be creative and use mint or coriander)

ROASTED PEPPERS

1 red or yellow pepper

2 cloves garlic, crushed

1 tsp capers, chopped

fresh oregano

TOMATOES

1 cup cherry tomatoes

1 Tbsp parsley, finely chopped

½ cup hummus (p. 23)*

ZUCCHINI

2 medium-sized zucchini

1 Tbsp chopped toasted walnuts

1 tsp chopped parsley

1 Tbsp vinaigrette

walnut oil

CURRIED MUSHROOMS

12 button mushrooms

1 tsp olive oil

1 tsp curry powder

1 Tbsp macadamia nuts, finely chopped

BAKED GARLIC

2–3 whole heads of garlic

EASY SUSHI

3 cups cooked brown rice

1 Tbsp rice vinegar

FILLINGS: (select one or more)

sliced avocado

pickled ginger

finely chopped red pepper

cut greens of a spring/green onion into 1 inch lengths

thin strips of sushi nori or similar

¼ carrot cut into matchsticks (1 inch long)

1 Tbsp roasted sliced seaweed (yakinori)

½ cup of marinated tofu, finely sliced

a few finely chopped greens of a spring /green onion

1 small cucumber cut into small cubes, leave some for fine julienned strips for garnishing

SERVES 12–14

For this recipe I use a rice cube. If you are unable to purchase one, then try the traditional method of rolling, using sushi nori and a bamboo sushi mat. I have provided a few vegetable items for you to include, using the easy sushi device. Feel free, however, to add other ingredients.

Place the cooked rice in a bowl and add the rice vinegar. Stir in well and leave to cool.

Choose a selection of one or more or all of the fillings or some of your own.

TO ASSEMBLE:

This is a great opportunity to encourage children to experiment with making their own sushi. You may be surprised with the results.

Try making your own version with whatever design and ingredients appeal to you. You are only limited by your own imagination when it comes to presenting these interesting lite bites. To make it easier, instructions come with the cube to give you a few basic ideas to start with. You can also refer to the photo for ideas on garnishing each sushi.

Makes about 12–14 sushi.

| PER SERVING | Calories 254 | Protein 7g | Fat 6g | Carbohydrates 43g | Sugar a3g | Fiber 5g | Sodium 90mg |

Rice Cube

ASIAN SPRING ROLLS GF

It is wise to prepare all ingredients before assembling rolls.

Cook noodles according to packet instructions.

Heat a saucepan or pot until medium-hot. Add the garlic and onion and continue to sauté (without oil) until onion is soft and translucent. Add a little water if the mixture looks like its burning.

Add carrot, celery, spring/green onions, bean sprouts, and cabbage and stir well for 1–2 mins or until vegetables appear limp but still al denté.

Add the cooked noodles, chestnuts, soy sauce, salt, sugar, coriander, and peanuts. Stir through gently and reheat briefly.

Add the dissolved cornstarch to mixture to thicken. At last, add ginger and distribute evenly through mixture. Put aside to cool.

TO ASSEMBLE:

Immerse each wrapper in warm water and soak for about 20–30 secs until softened. Remove from water and allow excess water to drip off. Place wrapper on damp tea towel and put 1 Tbsp of the mixture onto the bottom ⅓ of wrapper. Roll the wrapper firmly (in envelope style) around the filling, slightly stretching the wrapper as you work to ensure a tight fit. Repeat process until all the filling is used.

Cover completed rolls with a damp tea towel to prevent them from drying out. Remove damp towel prior to serving.

Serve immediately with a dipping sauce (p. 87).

Makes about 10–12 spring rolls.

TIP: Rice wrappers for this recipe can be obtained from most supermarkets and Asian stores.

1 cup fine rice noodles

1 clove garlic, crushed

1 onion, finely chopped

1 cup carrot,
cut into straws 1½ inches long

1 cup celery
cut into straws 1½–2 inches long

½ cup spring/green onions,
chopped

½ cup bean sprouts

1 cup finely chopped
cabbage leaves

4–5 water chestnuts,
coarsely chopped

1 Tbsp light soy sauce or tamari

1 tsp brown sugar

1 cup coriander leaves,
coarsely chopped

2 Tbsp peanuts,
toasted and chopped

1 Tbsp cornstarch
mixed with 3 Tbsp water

1 Tbsp pickled ginger

10–12 rice wrappers

SERVES 10

PER SERVING   Calories 204   Protein 6g   Fat 4g   Carbohydrates 36g   Sugar 8g   Fiber 5g   Sodium 435mg

GRILLED WATERMELON WITH TOMATO AND PISTACHIO

18 oz fresh young watermelon

4 firm tomatoes skinned, deseeded, and chopped

¼ cup chopped and toasted pistachio nuts

1 small bunch of basil leaves

SERVES 4

Looks great on the plate and makes a nice appetizing tasty bite. Make sure your watermelon is young and fresh.

To grill segments of watermelon, cut into even sections—3 inches by 2 inches by 1 inch thick. Place "fingers" on a hot grilling plate. Turn when the underside is chargrilled and patterned black.

Place on a serving plate. (These fingers can also be "fried" in a hot fry pan for a few minutes until lightly charred.)

Place 1–2 tsp of chopped tomatoes on top of each chargrilled watermelon finger then sprinkle with a few chopped pistachios. Dress with some finely chopped basil. Serve immediately.

TIP: When roasting pistachio nuts place them in a slow oven at 255°F for about 10–15 mins. A slow oven allows the nuts to roast gently all the way through. Don't expose them to direct heat as they will burn and become bitter to taste.

PER SERVING	Calories 140	Protein 10g	Fat 6g	Carbohydrates 11g	Sugar 10g	Fiber 3	Sodium 8mg

WATERMELON— SYNONYMOUS WITH SUMMER AND PICNICS

"If you don't take care of your body, where are you going to live?" ANONYMOUS

FRUIT GAZPACHO

2 lb young watermelon

¼ cantaloupe

¼ honeydew melon

1 cup pineapple
cut into ½ inch cubes

2 kiwi fruit, peeled and
coarsely chopped

2 oranges cut into ½ inch
pieces

pulp of 4 passionfruit

1 cup strawberries,
quartered or halved

3 Tbsp lemon juice

2 tsp maple syrup (optional)

SERVES 6

*This becomes a conversation piece when served chilled as a first
course on those hot summer days. Other seasonal fruit could replace
some of the items.*

Peel the watermelon and cut into sizes that pass into a blender, juicer
or juice extractor (2 lb watermelon makes about 4 cups of juice).
Blend well, then strain juice through a cheesecloth.

Using a small melon ball tool, make as many melon balls as you can
obtain from the cantaloupe and honeydew. Any unused fruit or extra
pineapple can be added to the juicer with the watermelon.

Combine fruit and spoon into serving glasses. Add lemon juice and
maple syrup to watermelon juice, stir and pour juice over to just below
the level of the fruit.

Serve chilled and garnish with a fanned strawberry or a couple of
raspberries and a sprig of mint.

PER SERVING	Calories 117	Protein 3g	Fat 1g	Carbohydrates 24g	Sugar 24g	Fiber 6g	Sodium 32mg

CUCUMBER SOUP

3 cloves garlic, crushed

1 medium-sized onion,
chopped

5 spring/green onions,
with the green tops

3 cups cucumbers, chopped

1 medium potato, chopped

5 cups water with 4 tsp
stock powder (see p. 83)

¼ cup coconut milk

¼ cup verjus (see p. 13)

SERVES 6

This is a great soup for those with an overabundance of cucumbers.

Sauté garlic and onions (without oil) for a few minutes in a medium-
hot saucepan or pot until onions are soft and transparent. Add spring/
green onions plus tops. Allow them to wilt and soften, will take only 1
min.

Add chopped cucumbers and potato. Stir mixture then add stock.
Cover and simmer for 20–30 mins until all vegetables are cooked
through.

Blend soup with a handheld blender or pour soup into a large
processor and blend until soup is smooth.

Add coconut milk and verjus, stir and heat gently for a few minutes
before serving.

This soup can be served hot or chilled with an ice cube.

*TIP: Peel cucumbers if the skins are of the hard-skin variety, otherwise
leave the skins on.*

PER SERVING	Calories 190	Protein 4g	Fat 2g	Carbohydrates 14g	Sugar 6g	Fiber 4g	Sodium 353mg

MUSHROOM SOUP (GF)

For those chilly winter evenings, here is a lovely satisfying soup.

Place all the vegetables in a large saucepan and add enough stock to cover. Add paprika and bring to heat. Simmer for 30 mins.

Finally add verjus and stir through. Bring back to heat.

Serve topped with parsley and/or tofu sour cream (p. 89).

2 cups per serving.

2 cups button mushrooms, chopped

1 small carrot, chopped

1 small onion, chopped

1 stalk of celery, chopped

½ tsp paprika

5 cups of water with 4 tsp stock powder (see p. 83)

2 Tbsp parsley

¼ cup verjus (see p. 13)

SERVES 6

PER SERVING   Calories 55   Protein 4g   Fat 2g   Carbohydrates 4g   Sugar 4g   Fiber 3g   Sodium 367mg

BEST SERVED WITH WARM CRUSTY BREAD

Soups can even
take the place
of a main meal
and are just as
nourishing.

"Genes are not your destiny."

N. BARNARD, MD

PUMPKIN SOUP

This soup is one my husband makes. It's a great favorite with the family and is a warm and filling winter soup especially when served with toast or croutons.

Sauté garlic and onion (without oil) in a hot saucepan. Stir constantly to prevent burning until onions are soft and translucent for about 2– 3 mins. Add 1 Tbsp water to prevent onions from burning.

Add cooked pumpkin, stock, lemon juice, cloves, sugar, and salt and simmer for 15 mins while stirring occasionally. Puree with a stick blender or blender. Bring soup back to a simmer and lastly add milk, then gently heat through before serving.

Top with a little tofu sour cream (p. 89) and chopped parsley. Makes 2 cups per serving.

TIP: I find roasted pumpkin has a richer flavor than steamed pumpkin.

* Nut parmesan may be obtained from some vegan restaurants.
It makes a nice substitute for parmesan cheese.

1 clove garlic, chopped

1 large onion, chopped

2 cups cooked and peeled pumpkin (Japanese if you can get it)

5 cups water with 4 tsp stock powder (p. 83)

2 tsp lemon juice

¼ tsp ground cloves

1 tsp brown sugar

1 cup nondairy milk (or further stock)

¼ cup verjus (see p. 13)

1 tsp nut parmesan* (optional)

SERVES 6

PER SERVING	Calories 100	Protein 5g	Fat 2g	Carbohydrates 15g	Sugar 11g	Fiber 4g	Sodium 372mg

LEEK AND POTATO SOUP (VICHYSSOISE) GF

For those hot summer days, serve it chilled with an ice cube in each plate.

Sauté onion and garlic (without oil) in a large hot saucepan and stir continuously for 30 secs or so adding 1–2 Tbsp hot water to prevent burning. Sauté gently until the onions are translucent and soft. Replace lid to prevent evaporation.

Add chopped leeks and stir well. Cook another 5 mins with the lid on firmly.

Add sliced potatoes and stock and simmer gently for another 20–25 mins until potatoes are tender and falling apart.

Blend in a processor or with a handheld blender until the soup is very smooth. Then add verjus. More stock may be added for a thinner consistency if desired. Bring to simmer again and serve with chopped chives and/or tofu sour cream (p. 89). Makes 2 cups per serving.

1 clove of garlic, finely chopped

1 onion, chopped

2 leeks, washed well and sliced with the green tops

3 large potatoes, peeled and finely sliced

5 cups water with 4 tsp stock powder (p. 83)

¼ cup verjus (p. 13)

3 Tbsp chives, chopped

SERVES 6

PER SERVING	Calories 95	Protein 5g	Fat 1g	Carbohydrates 16g	Sugar 8g	Fiber 5g	Sodium 367mg

REFRESHING WHEN SERVED CHILLED IN SUMMER

Salads & Sides

The following recipes may be served as a single course, an entrée, or offered as an accompaniment to one of the main dishes in the next section.

GREEN MANGOES TASTE SWEET AND SOUR AND CARRY FLAVORS WELL.

"There is no 'good' cholesterol in foods."

N. BARNARD, MD

GARDEN SALAD

3½ oz lettuce mix

5 oz cherry tomatoes

1 cucumber, finely sliced

6 baby beets

2 zucchini

1 avocado

¼ carrot

VINAIGRETTE

¼ cup lemon juice

2 tsp olive oil

1 clove garlic, crushed

pinch of salt

1 tsp brown sugar

SERVES 4

You are only limited by your imagination and the salad items in your fridge when it comes to creating a garden salad. Here is a simple salad that can be put together in minutes.

Toss lettuce, tomatoes, and cucumber together and arrange on a serving platter. Carefully position baby beets on salad.

Using a potato peeler or mandarin, slice zucchini lengthwise and place into boiling water for 2 mins. Remove and plunge slices into iced water to refresh. Set aside for 5 mins then roll into curls and add them to the salad.

Peel avocado and slice thinly from base almost through to stalk end. Place on center of dish and fan avocado out. Garnish with carrot curls and a light dressing.

VINAIGRETTE

Place ingredients in a screw top jar and shake well or blend with a stick blender.

Serve separately in a small bowl. Makes ¹⁄₃ cup.

PER SERVING	Calories 147	Protein 6g	Fat 7g	Carbohydrates 15g	Sugar 14g	Fiber 8g	Sodium 231mg

GREEN MANGO SALAD

2 green mangoes,*
finely shredded**

2 red onions, finely sliced

1 medium beet, finely sliced into 1 inch long matchsticks

1 or 2 small green chile, deseeded and finely chopped

2 oz coriander leaves, roughly chopped

1 Tbsp low-salt soy sauce

2 tsp palm sugar

6 Tbsp strained lime juice

2 Tbsp fresh orange juice, strained

SERVES 4

Green mangoes are used widely in Asian cuisine and have a pleasant lemony flavor. (See image on opposite page.)

Toss all the salad ingredients including chile, and coriander, together carefully to combine. Be mindful that fresh beets can "bleed" into other ingredients, so take care not to disturb the salad too much once beets is added.

Then whisk soy sauce, sugar, lime, and orange juices together to combine. Taste and adjust seasoning if required and pour over the mixed salad just before serving.

* Ask at your Asian suppliers or fruit market for green mangoes.

** To shred mango into fine strips: first peel them, then hold the peeled mango in the palm of one hand. Using a sharp edged knife cut very fine narrow deep cuts toward the seed while continuing to turn the fruit, then using a potato peeler, "shave" lengthwise down the cuts made with the knife. This will then give you the long fine shreds preferred for this salad.

PER SERVING	Calories 141	Protein 4g	Fat 1g	Carbohydrates 29g	Sugar 27g	Fiber 7g	Sodium 237mg

WALDORF SALAD GF

You will love this salad.

Dice apples and add lemon juice to prevent discoloration. Add celery, drained pineapple, raisins, and toasted walnuts.

Add lemon juice or mayonnaise and stir through the salad.

Spoon into a serving bowl lined with mixed lettuce leaves and garnish with a few dried cranberries.

TIP: When toasting walnuts place them in a slow oven at 255°F for about 10–15 mins. A slow oven allows the nuts to toast gently all the way through.

Drizzle with lemon juice or 1/2 cup tofu mayonnaise (p. 88). Both work well with this salad.

3 red apples, cut into ½ inch cubes

1 Tbsp lemon juice

2 stalks celery, cut into ½ inch lengths

1½ cups fresh pineapple, cut into 1 inch cubes or 1 can pineapple pieces in natural juice, well drained

¼ cup raisins

1 cup of toasted walnuts chopped

3 Tbsp lemon juice or ½ cup tofu mayonnaise (p. 88)

1 Tbsp dried cranberries (optional)

SERVES 4

PER SERVING	Calories 225	Protein 3g	Fat 5g	Carbohydrates 42g	Sugar 39g	Fiber 7g	Sodium 27mg

COLESLAW GF

One of my favorite coleslaw recipes.

Shred cabbage finely with a mandolin or with a very sharp knife. Place celery, apples, grapes, and walnuts (reserve 1 Tbsp walnuts for garnishing) in a large bowl and toss well to combine. Add lemon juice or mayonnaise to salad and combine well. Serve mounded on a serving platter and top with remaining walnuts. Garnish with a sprig of parsley or mint.

¼ white cabbage

2 celery stalks, finely sliced

1 green apple, diced

1 red apple, diced

¾ cup green or black grapes

½ cup walnuts, toasted and chopped

3 Tbsp lemon juice or ¼ cup tofu mayonnaise (p. 88)

SERVES 4

PER SERVING	Calories 102	Protein 3g	Fat 2g	Carbohydrates 18g	Sugar 18g	Fiber 6g	Sodium 39mg

ORANGE AND DATE SALAD GF

4 large or 6 medium oranges,
peeled with pith removed

1–2 tsp castor sugar

2 medium-sized lemons, juiced

4–5 dates, chopped finely

2–3 Tbsp almonds,
slivered or flaked

1 tsp cinnamon powder (p. 13)

1–2 mint sprigs

SERVES 4

This is my husband's recipe, which he executes well. Looks impressive on a flat platter when dressed and tastes equally as nice.

Finely slice the peeled oranges and arrange slices on a flat oval white serving dish (like the scales on a fish).

Add sugar to the lemon juice and stir until thoroughly mixed and dissolved. Set aside.

Sprinkle chopped dates down the center of the orange slices and add the slivered/flaked almonds over the top. Drizzle the lemon juice/sugar over the oranges. Lastly, lightly sprinkle cinnamon over the whole dish.

Garnish with torn mint leaves.

| PER SERVING | Calories 106 | Protein 3g | Fat 1g | Carbohydrates 21g | Sugar 21g | Fiber 7g | Sodium 6mg |

4 large potatoes, peeled

1 small onion, finely chopped

½ green pepper, chopped

2 Tbsp tofu mayonnaise

2 tsp whole black peppercorns

2 tsp of micro herbs

SERVES 4

MAYONNAISE

½ cup of silken tofu

1 small pinch salt

1 tsp lemon juice

¼ tsp Dijon mustard

¼ tsp honey

freshly ground black pepper
to taste

POTATO SALAD GF

There are many ways of putting potato salad together. This is my favorite, which works well for our family.

Cut potatoes into 1 inch cubes and steam over boiling water for 20 mins until cooked through. Cool before placing in a mixing bowl. Add the onion, green pepper, and mayonnaise and mix in.

Garnish with black peppercorns and sprigs of micro herbs or finely chopped parsley.

MAYONNAISE

Place all ingredients in a blender and process until smooth and creamy (about 5 mins).

Serve chilled. Will keep up to a week when stored covered in the refrigerator.

| PER SERVING | Calories 132 | Protein 16g | Fat 3g | Carbohydrates 8g | Sugar 7g | Fiber 4g | Sodium 51mg |

ORANGE, ALMOND, AND SAFFRON COUS COUS

This is a most interesting dish with an orange juice reduction.

Bring the freshly squeezed orange juice to a boil in a pan over medium to high heat. Reduce to low heat and simmer gently for 18—20 mins until the juice has reduced to about ¾ cup syrupy juice, watching carefully should it look like bubbling over.

Add mustard, ginger, cumin, and saffron-infused stock to the hot reduced orange juice. Mix well and bring to a simmer.

Place cous cous and salt in a bowl, then pour the sauce over the cous cous. Stir, then cover bowl with plastic wrap and let stand for 10 mins or until stock is absorbed.

Fluff cous cous with a fork. Then mix in the salt, oil, lemon juice, and ground peppercorns to taste.

Just before serving, fold in the almonds, chopped coriander and mint, and transfer to a serving bowl.

TIP: To toast almonds place in a preheated oven at 250°F for 10 mins, then allow to cool.

*See p. 13 for how to cook with saffron.

2 cups fresh orange juice, strained

2 tsp Dijon mustard

2 tsp fresh ginger, grated

½ tsp cumin, freshly ground

1½ cups hot vegetable stock (add grated zest of 1 large orange, a pinch of saffron threads,* and infuse for 15 mins)

1½ cups cous cous

1 tsp salt

2 tsp extra virgin olive oil

2 Tbsp lemon juice

1 pinch freshly ground black peppercorns

1 Tbsp almonds, flaked and toasted

½ cup each fresh coriander and mint, chopped

SERVES 4

PER SERVING	Calories 318	Protein 12g	Fat 2g	Carbohydrates 63g	Sugar 14g	Fiber 8g	Sodium 198mg

DATE AND ORANGE COUS COUS SALAD

1½ cups whole grain cous cous

2 cups water with
1½ tsp stock powder (p. 83)

1 red apple,
peeled, cored, and diced

1 small carrot, cut into fine
matchsticks, 1 inch long

½ cup dates,
pitted and chopped

¼ cup sultanas (raisins)

½ cup hazelnuts,
toasted and chopped

1 Tbsp orange rind,
finely grated

2 tsp mint, chopped

ORANGE DRESSING

⅓ cup fresh orange juice

2 Tbsp lemon juice

1 tsp olive oil

2 tsp honey

SERVES 4

I have made this dish several times and it is always well received by family and friends. The orange dressing adds a lovely citrus flavor to the dish.

Place cous cous in a medium-sized bowl and add hot stock. Cover bowl with plastic wrap and set aside for 5 mins until water is absorbed, then stir well with a fork to fluff up grains.

Add all other ingredients to cous cous except mint and toss well.

Place dressing ingredients in a small mixing bowl and whisk together. Drizzle dressing over the salad just prior to serving and decorate with mint.

PER SERVING   Calories 555   Protein 12g   Fat 7g   Carbohydrates 86g   Sugar 36g   Fiber 9g   Sodium 224mg

MOROCCAN COUS COUS

Use the larger Israeli or pearl cous cous for this tasty dish.
I know you will enjoy this recipe.

Bring the water, stock, and Mediterranean seasoning to a simmer and add cous cous.

Gently cook for 8–10 mins until the grains are soft and water is mostly absorbed. Fork through to ensure the grains are separated. Cover and set aside.

Sauté garlic and onion (without oil) in a hot pan stirring constantly, add water as needed to prevent burning, until the onion becomes soft and transparent—about 1–2 mins.

Add the fennel, cumin seeds, rasins. Then add the pepper, stir well and cook over a low heat for another 5–7 mins. You may need to add the extra stock at this stage to keep mixture moist. Turn off heat.

Stir in the spinach until it wilts (30 secs) then add the cous cous and almonds. Mix in well. Add additional stock if cous cous looks dry.

Lastly, add the parsley and coriander and stir in gently. Spoon mixture into a warmed serving bowl and serve immediately.

2 ¼ cups water with 2 tsp stock powder (p. 83)

1 tsp mild Mediterranean seasoning

¾ cup Moroccan (pearl) cous cous

2 cloves garlic, chopped

1 large onion, chopped

1 Tbsp fennel seeds

1 Tbsp cumin seeds

1 Tbsp sultanas (raisins)

1 red pepper, chopped

3.5 oz baby spinach leaves, stalks removed

2 Tbsp slivered almonds

2 handfuls fresh parsley, chopped

1 handful fresh coriander, chopped

¼ cup extra stock (optional)

SERVES 4

PER SERVING	Calories 295	Protein 14g	Fat 5g	Carbohydrates 63g	Sugar 11g	Fiber 7g	Sodium 348mg

QUINOA AND AVOCADO TIMBALES

½ cup quinoa

1½ cups water with 1 tsp stock powder (p. 83)

1 cup of finely diced eggplant

½ cup water with ¼ tsp stock powder

2 cucumbers, finely diced

2 tomatoes, blanched, skinned, deseeded and finely chopped

½ cup parsley, finely chopped

2 Tbsp lemon juice

1 small handful of basil leaves chopped

1 firm avocado, cut into small thin pieces for garnishing

4 SERVES

Timbales, specially the cone shape, add visual appeal to a plate when served as an entree with a small side salad. The timbale needs to be tightly packed to retain it's shape after removal from the mold. Cous cous works just as well with this recipe.

Place quinoa in a small saucepan with 1½ cups of stock and bring to a boil then reduce to a simmer, cover and cook for 15–20 mins, until all the stock is absorbed. Remove from heat and set aside to cool and for grains to continue drying out.

Cook eggplant gently in the remaining ½ cup stock for 20 mins or so until soft. Cover and set aside to cool. Drain diced cucumber on paper towels.

When the quinoa is cooked and cooled, combine all ingredients together including the basil.

Fill the timbale (metal cone). Pack firmly. Up end the timbale on a serving plate, tap base of cone for easier removal of contents. Dress with avocado, a sprig of basil or micro herbs, and a light citrus dressing around the base of each timbale.

Continue the process until all the mixture is used.

Depending on size of mold, there is enough for 6–8 timbales.

TIP: Timbale (cone) is a mold for shaping food. Wet the cone before filling, as it is easier to remove.

Variation: Replace eggplant with roasted yellow pepper if preferred.

PER SERVING	Calories 210	Protein 13g	Fat 6g	Carbohydrates 18g	Sugar 6g	Fiber 5g	Sodium 214mg

TIMBALE – A MOLD FOR FOOD PRESENTATION

CHESTNUT AND POTATO MASH

Wonderful when chestnuts are in season but if not, use the canned variety. This mash is very nice as an accompaniment for steamed vegetables, for entrees, or instead of sauces. The only disadvantage is the time it takes to prepare the fresh chestnuts for cooking, a time consuming task but worth it in the end.

If using fresh chestnuts, cut a slash in the skin of each nut and cook in a saucepan of boiling water for about 5 mins. Remove pan from heat. Lift a few chestnuts at a time from the water and peel off the outer skin and the thin inner one.

Simmer peeled chestnuts, chopped potatoes, and lemon peel in the milk for about 15–20 mins or until tender.

Remove lemon peel. Drain the cooked chestnuts and potatoes, reserving any milk. Pass through a coarse sieve into a bowl or blend well in a food processor.

Place over a low heat and beat in the reserved milk until a fluffy, smooth mixture is obtained. Add honey and season with salt and ground pepper and serve. Serve as a base for patties.

Tip: May also be served with a drizzle of caper rosemary oil (p. 86).

2 cups fresh chestnuts (canned if fresh are not available)

3 medium potatoes, chopped

2 slices lemon peel

1–2 cups nondairy milk

2 tsp honey

½ tsp salt

1 pinch freshly ground black peppercorns

SERVES 6

PER SERVING	Calories 262	Protein 15g	Fat 4g	Carbohydrates 46g	Sugar 10g	Fiber 19g	Sodium 230mg

CELERIAC MASH

This is another surprisingly successful alternative to mashed potatoes and is a great way to try celeriac for the first time. It is most acceptable when served with your choice of pattie. Although celeriac is a largely underrated vegetable, it can be used in a variety of ways—this is just one of them. Works well when served with a few drops of caper rosemary oil (p. 89).

Put the celeriac and potatoes into a medium-sized saucepan with thyme and lemon zest. Add sufficient milk to just cover. Bring to a boil and simmer vegetables gently over a low heat for about 20–25 mins or until tender. Remove thyme and lemon zest.

Drain well (reserving ½ cup of the milk). Pass the vegetables through a sieve into a clean saucepan or blend well in a food processor.

Reheat very gently. Stir in reserved milk and mix in well. More milk may be required for desired soft consistency. Add spring/green onion to finished puree and combine.

Season with salt and freshly ground peppercorns to taste.

2 cups celeriac, peeled and cut into chunks

2 medium-sized potatoes, peeled and chopped

1 sprig thyme

1 strip lemon zest

15–20 oz nondairy milk

1 finely sliced spring /green onion

½ tsp salt

1 pinch freshly ground black peppercorns

SERVES 6

PER SERVING	Calories 94	Protein 10g	Fat 2g	Carbohydrates 9g	Sugar 6g	Fiber 5g	Sodium 152mg

BRUSSELS SPROUTS WITH MACADAMIA CRUMBS

Brussels sprouts with a difference.

2 cups sprouts,
trimmed and halved

¼ cup day-old, whole-grain
breadcrumbs / rye coarse
breadcrumbs

1 clove garlic, crushed

¼ tsp salt

¼ cup roasted macadamia
nuts, finely chopped

1 Tbsp olive oil

2 Tbsp lemon juice

2–3 tsp chopped parsley

SERVES 4

Steam brussels sprouts for 10–12 mins or until tender. Remove from steamer, set aside, and keep warm.

Place the breadcrumbs and garlic in a bowl, add salt and chopped macadamias. Mix ingredients together.

Place oil in a medium-hot frying pan and add the crumbs. Fry for 3–4 mins stirring until nicely golden and crispy.

Add the lemon juice to brussels sprouts and stir gently to ensure they are well coated.

Place brussels sprouts and any left over lemon juice in a serving dish, sprinkle the crumbs over the sprouts and garnish with chopped parsley. Serve warm.

TIP: To reduce cooking time, cut sprouts in half. They are just as nice when halved and it seems to make the dish go further.

PER SERVING	Calories 188	Protein 7g	Fat 8g	Carbohydrates 22g	Sugar 3g	Fiber 6g	Sodium 274mg

KALE AND TOFU SALAD (P. 51)

CHARGRILLED POLENTA WITH GF TOMATOES AND BASIL

A very tasty dish, popular in the Owens family. Has great eye appeal when served on a platter or on individual plates

Bring stock to a boil in a saucepan. Remove from heat and slowly add the polenta a little at a time (whisking well to prevent lumps from forming) until all the polenta has been added. Continue stirring over a gentle simmer for a minute or two until the polenta is cooked and mixture is thick. Stir in nutritional yeast flakes and mix in evenly.

Spoon the cooked polenta into a nonstick baking pan (8×6 3-inch), line pan with parchment paper. Level and smooth the surface using a wet spatula. Refrigerate for 1 hr until completely cooled and set.

Heat a grilling plate or frying pan until medium-hot.

Turn polenta out and brush both sides very lightly with oil. Cut into 10–12 triangles or "fingers." Place polenta shapes onto the hot grilling plate or frying pan and cook for several minutes on each side until lightly charred and crisp.

Arrange on a serving platter and keep warm in an oven on low heat.

Variations:

1. Arrange the 10–12 chargrilled triangles or "fingers" on a warmed serving platter and scatter chargrilled cherry tomatoes over the top. Add the crumbled feta and garnish with torn mint leaves.

2. Spread ½ tsp of basil pesto onto each round chargrilled polenta shape (see photo), add a tsp of diced tomatoes, cucumber, crumbled feta, and garnish with mint sprigs. Serve immediately.

4 cups water with 3 tsp stock powder (p. 83)

1¼ cups polenta

2 Tbsp nutritional yeast flakes

1 tsp olive oil

2 Tbsp basil pesto (p. 87) (optional)

12 cherry tomatoes, chargrilled or 3 finely diced tomatoes

¼ cup cucumber, finely diced

¼ cup mint leaves, coarsely torn

1 Tbsp nondairy feta

SERVES 4

PER SERVING   Calories 256   Protein 11g   Fat 4g   Carbohydrates 44g   Sugar 2g   Fiber 5g   Sodium 497mg

---

TRADITIONAL TABOULEH

I've seen this served with pomegranate seeds. They give a lovely color to the dish when a ¼ cup of pomegranate seeds is spooned through and some sprinkled on top before serving. Try replacing bulgur wheat with cooked quinoa. It's a great option to try.

Place bulgur wheat in a bowl and add boiling water. Cover and let stand for 35 mins until tender and liquid is absorbed. Drain well by squeezing out excess water through a cheesecloth.

Place in a bowl with remaining ingredients. Mix well.

SERVES 4

1 cup bulgur wheat
2 cups boiling water
4 oz cherry tomatoes, quartered
1 medium cucumber, finely chopped
1 clove garlic, crushed
1 cup fresh parsley, chopped
½ cup fresh mint, chopped
3 spring/green onions, thinly sliced
2 Tbsp lemon zest
2 Tbsp lemon juice
2 tsp olive oil
½ tsp salt
1 pinch freshly ground black peppercorns

PER SERVING   Calories 91   Protein 3g   Fat 3g   Carbohydrates 13g   Sugar 4g   Fiber 5g   Sodium 325mg

---

SERVE WITH POMEGRANATE SEEDS FOR VISUAL APPEAL

ASPARAGUS GF

Asparagus can be cooked in different ways.
Here is my preferred cooking method.

Snap stems to remove lower fibrous part. Wash asparagus and peel lower stems lightly with a potato peeler if needed.

Trim asparagus to an even length. Immerse asparagus in a large pan with simmering salted water. Bring pan back to heat and simmer for 3 mins until spears turn bright green. Remove pan from heat and allow to stand for another 3 mins. Drain spears and plunge them into ice water for several minutes to halt further cooking and to retain the color. Drain well.

Sprinkle lemon juice and some salt over the asparagus for extra flavor. When serving spears (like soldiers, side by side, facing the same way) with béchamel sauce, spoon sauce across the center of the stems prior to serving on a platter.

Garnish with a few sprigs of thyme and 1 or 2 halved cherry tomatoes.

BÉCHAMEL SAUCE

This sauce is very versatile and can be used when making lasagne or other pasta dishes.

Drain cashews and set aside.

Place the garlic and cashews in a small blender and blend until paste. Add yeast flakes, lemon juice, potato starch or cornstarch, onion flakes, and a little stock to the blender and blend well. Add the remaining stock slowly and blend for a few more seconds.

Pour into a saucepan and bring to simmer while stirring continuously until mixture starts to thicken. Add nondairy milk or additional water for the consistency required. Add a few grinds of salt and a little freshly ground black peppercorn. Do not boil.

Serve with vegetables. Makes about 1½ cups.

4 bunches fresh green asparagus

1 Tbsp lemon juice

1 cup béchamel sauce (optional)

BÉCHAMEL SAUCE

¼ cup cashews, soaked in hot water for 30 mins

1 clove garlic, crushed

1 Tbsp nutritional yeast flakes

1 tsp lemon juice

2 tsp potato starch or cornstarch, mixed with 2 Tbsp cold water

½ tsp onion flakes

½ tsp salt

1 ¾ cups water with 1 ½ tsp stock powder (p. 83)

1 freshly ground black peppercorn to taste

SERVES 6

PER SERVING	Calories 55	Protein 4g	Fat 3g	Carbohydrates 3g	Sugar 2g	Fiber 2g	Sodium 90mg

LIMA BEAN CASSEROLE GF

Dorothy Clarke

13 oz dried lima beans
(about 4½ cups when soaked)

1 small onion

3 bay leaves

1 tsp honey

½ cup of light coconut milk

½ tsp salt

½ cup chopped parsley

SERVES 4

To save time, use your pressure cooker for the lima beans. The aroma in this dish from the cloves and bay leaves is amazing! Instructions on cooking beans are found on p. 9.

Cook beans for about 4–6 mins on high pressure (or according to your pressure cooker instructions) with the onion and bay leaves.

Drain beans and place into a bowl. Remove onion and bay leaves.

Add honey, salt, and enough coconut milk and water to obtain the desired consistency. Add the chopped parsley and stir well yet gently.

Garnish with a sprig of parsley.

PER SERVING	Calories 288	Protein 23g	Fat 4g	Carbohydrates 49g	Sugar 6g	Fiber 12g	Sodium 287mg

TOMATO, ROAST PUMPKIN, AND MINT SALSA GF

¼ pumpkin roasted

2 firm ripe tomatoes, diced

1 cucumber, chopped

1 medium red onion, finely sliced

¼ cup mint leaves, chopped

1 Tbsp lime or lemon juice

¼ cup green olives,
coarsely chopped

1 tsp honey

¼ cup parsley,
finely chopped

1 tsp red chile, finely sliced
and deseeded (optional)

SERVES 4

This is nice served alongside dips or served as an accompaniment to most of the patties in this book.

Cut pumpkin into 1¼ inch cubes, place onto an oven tray lined with parchment paper and bake in a pre-heated oven at 350°F for 30–40 mins or until pumpkin is cooked.

Allow to cool before adding all the other ingredients.

PER SERVING	Calories 74	Protein 3g	Fat 2g	Carbohydrates 11g	Sugar 9g	Fiber 4g	Sodium 111mg

CHILE BEANS

This recipe with its mildly hot accent may be served warm with burritos, shredded lettuce, tomatoes, grated carrots, etc., and a tofu sour cream (p.89).

For cooking dried beans see p. 9. When cooked, remove bay leaves and onion.

Place TVP in a bowl with boiling stock and allow to "steam." Cover and let stand for 5 mins then drain any excess stock and set aside.

Sauté chiles (without oil). Stir lightly for 30 secs. Add the onion and cook until transparent, stirring continuously—add some water to prevent burning, as needed. Cook gently for 2 mins then add the peppers, stir in well and cook another 2–3 mins.

Lastly, add tomatoes and TVP. Simmer for another 2–3 mins.

Place all ingredients in a covered casserole dish and bake in a preheated oven at 350°F for 30–40 mins.

Tip: A pressure cooker will come in handy when preparing this dish.

1½ cups dried red kidney beans

1 cup TVP (textured vegetable protein) (p. 13)

1¼ cups water with 1 tsp stock powder (p. 83)

3 small red chiles, deseeded and finely chopped

1 medium onion, chopped

1 medium red pepper, chopped

1 green pepper, chopped

2× 14 oz canned or 28 oz fresh tomatoes, peeled and chopped

SERVES 4

PER SERVING	Calories 407	Protein 33g	Fat 7g	Carbohydrates 53g	Sugar 13g	Fiber 12g	Sodium 169mg

DHAL

If you like a spicy dhal as I do, then try this recipe. Serve on the side with vegetable curry (p. 66).

Sauté onion, garlic, and ginger (without oil), add 2 Tbsp water to prevent burning if needed, until soft and translucent. Add chile, turmeric, cardamom, and cumin seeds.

Cook for a another 2 mins then add lentils and combine.

Gradually add the stock and bring to a boil. Simmer for 20–30 mins. If desired, add more stock. Add any optional extras during cooking.

*Optional extras: chopped tomatoes, shredded spinach, carrot or potato—cubed. Leave tomato and spinach until last 10 mins before adding to mixture.

1 onion, chopped

2 garlic cloves, finely chopped

2 inches fresh ginger, grated

½–1 tsp chile flakes, soaked in hot water for 15 mins and drained

1 tsp turmeric

1 tsp cardamom seeds

1 tsp cumin seeds

1 cup red lentils, soaked for 30 mins in hot water, rinsed and drained

2–2½ cups of water with 2 tsp stock powder (p. 83)

SERVES 4

PER SERVING	Calories 177	Protein 13g	Fat 2g	Carbohydrates 29g	Sugar 3g	Fiber 5g	Sodium 274mg

POTATO WEDGES

4 medium-large baking potatoes

2 Tbsp dukkah (p. 81)

2 tsp olive oil

SERVES 4

Use a small amount of oil.

Preheat the oven to 440°F .

Scrub potatoes well and steam until they are partially cooked (about 10 mins). Cut each potato into 6 or 7 wedges and dry well with paper towels.

Rub oil on the potato wedges by using disposable plastic gloves. Sprinkle with dukkah and coat potatoes well.

Place wedges on an oven tray lined with parchment paper and put prepared potatoes in the hot oven for 40 mins until tender and golden.

Serve immediately. Best served with Tofu Sour Cream (p. 89).

TIP: Choose potatoes with a floury texture that absorb little moisture such as russet sebago. Microwaving potatoes in their skins for 7–8 mins ensures the wedges are lovely and crisp on the outside with soft centers after roasting. Don't forget to fork the potatoes before microwaving.

PER SERVING	Calories 204	Protein 24g	Fat 8g	Carbohydrates 9g	Sugar 8g	Fiber 6g	Sodium 8mg

KALE AND TOFU SALAD

10 oz firm tofu

2 cups prepared kale, packed generously

2 cups red cabbage, finely sliced

1 Tbsp lime juice

1 cup snow peas

2 medium-sized carrots, cut into 1 inch length batons

2 Tbsp peanuts, chopped

MARINADE

1 Tbsp sweet chile sauce

3 Tbsp lime or lemon juice

2 tsp palm sugar, grated

1 tsp light soy sauce

1 clove garlic, crushed

SERVES 4

When using kale, a nutrient-rich vegetable, be sure you remove all the white ribs and then cut the remaining leaves into bite-sized pieces.

Prepare the marinade by combining sweet chile, lime juice, sugar, soy sauce, and garlic in a bowl.

Cut tofu into 1 inch cubes and add to the marinade. Gently coat all the tofu pieces, cover, and leave to refrigerate overnight.

Place the kale in a large bowl with the red cabbage and add lime juice. Combine well.

Slice the snow peas diagonally and add together with the carrot batons to the cabbage and kale. Next drain the tofu and add to the salad mix. Stir in gently.

Place in a serving bowl or platter, and sprinkle the peanuts over the salad. I find adding a few tsp of the marinade to the salad before serving adds a nice zing.

Finally garnish with chopped coriander or parsley.

(See page 45 for image.)

PER SERVING	Calories 193	Protein 14g	Fat 9g	Carbohydrates 14g	Sugar 13g	Fiber 10g	Sodium 246mg

Mains

Dishes served for the main course need to be interesting, full of flavor, as colorful as possible, and attractively plated. If one manages to accomplish most of these, guests will hardly notice the absence of meat and dairy, and they will enjoy a completely plant-based meal.

A DELIGHTFUL SPECIAL OCCASION DISH

"He who does not know food, how can he understand the diseases of man?"
HIPPOCRATES (THE FATHER OF MEDICINE)

TOFU AND VEGETABLE LATTICE FLAN

This is our daughter Sarah's recipe. Serve in small slices as this is a special occasion dish.

PASTRY:

1 cup whole wheat or spelt flour

2 Tbsp oil

1 tsp salt

¼ cup water

FILLING:

2 cloves garlic, crushed

1 cup onion, finely chopped

1 cup pepper, diced

1 cup carrots, diced

1 cup celery, diced

1 cup corn niblets

BLENDED INGREDIENTS:

1 cup cashews,
soaked in hot water for 30 mins

3 Tbsp nutritional yeast flakes

1 tsp stock powder (p. 83)

3 Tbsp cornstarch

10 oz silken tofu

1 tsp sweet basil

GARNISH:

1 red pepper,
roasted and skin removed

1 Tbsp pitted black olives

SERVES 8

PASTRY:

Mix the oil and salt together, add to flour with water. Mix until thoroughly combined. Refrigerate for 30 mins before pressing into rectangular flan pan 13½ × 5 inch. Bake in a preheated oven at 350°F for 10 mins. Allow to cool.

FILLING:

Sauté all these ingredients for 5–6 mins until cooked. Set aside.

BLENDED INGREDIENTS:

Process all these ingredients until smooth and creamy. Add to the sautéed vegetables and combine. Spoon into pastry lined flan tin. Bake in oven at 350°F for 30 mins then remove.

GARNISHING:

Halve pepper, remove seeds and white membranes. Bake in a preheated oven at 400°F for about 40 mins until soft and cooked. Place in a bowl, cover, and set aside to cool. Cut into 4–5 inch fine strips.

Arrange pepper strips to form a lattice pattern on surface of partially cooked flan. Return flan to oven and continue to cook for another 15 mins or until firm to touch.

Remove from oven and add the halved olives, round side up in the center of each diamond (see photo).

Garnish with parsley and cherry tomato.

PER SERVING   Calories 267   Protein 10g   Fat 15g   Carbohydrates 23g   Sugar 5g   Fiber 8g   Sodium 338mg

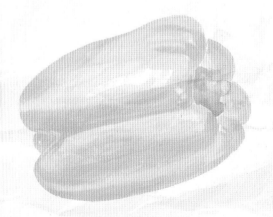

TOMATO VEGETABLE LOAF

Here is one of my all time favorites that I cook in a terrine. It may be served hot with sauce, sliced cold with salads, deep frozen, or made into patties by adding breadcrumbs and mashed potato. It freezes well for up to 2 weeks and looks impressive when garnished imaginatively with carrot, parsley, or olives.

Using a large mixing bowl add the breadcrumbs, chopped walnuts, salt, mixed herbs and stir through. Add the onion, finely blended carrots and celery.

Blend tomatoes with cornstarch and water until smooth. Add to mixture and stir all the ingredients well. Add extra water to obtain a softer consistency if desired.

Spoon into a terrine lined with parchment paper. Cover with the terrine lid.

Bake dish in a preheated oven at 350°F for 1¼ hr.

Allow to cool completely before turning loaf out onto a serving platter. Serve with gravy or sauce.

Garnish with parsley sprigs, cherry tomatoes, carrot, or zucchini curls.

¾ cup (6oz) whole wheat breadcrumbs

1 cup mixed nuts, finely chopped

½ tsp salt

1 tsp mixed herbs

1 onion, finely chopped

2 carrots, finely blended or minced

3 stalks celery, finely blended or minced

1 can tomatoes or 450g fresh tomatoes

2 Tbsp cornstarch, mixed with 6 Tbsp water

SERVES 6

PER SERVING	Calories 280	Protein 18g	Fat 11g	Carbohydrates 30g	Sugar 9g	Fiber 5g	Sodium 307mg

BEST SERVED WITH ROASTED RED PEPPER SAUCE (P. 86)

SPAGHETTI BOLOGNESE

14 oz whole grain
or spelt spaghetti

BOLOGNESE SAUCE:

3 cloves garlic, crushed

1 large onion, chopped

2 Tbsp tomato paste

15 oz fresh tomatoes, chopped

1 red or green pepper, chopped

1¼ cups hot water with 1 tsp
stock powder (p. 83)

1 cup TVP,* minced (optional)

2 Tbsp fresh thyme

2 Tbsp fresh oregano

¼ packed cup parsley

1 Tbsp nondairy cheese

SERVES 4

The secret of a good sauce is in long slow cooking and the use of fresh herbs. Nut parmesan may be found in vegan restaurants to replace parmesan cheese.

Reconstitute TVP.*

Sauté garlic and onion (without oil) in a hot pan, stirring constantly until onion becomes soft and translucent (2–3 mins).

Add tomato paste, fresh tomatoes, pepper, stock, reconstituted TVP, and fresh herbs. Stir well, cover and bring back to heat then simmer very gently for about 1 hr.

Meanwhile, using another saucepan, add 16–21 cups of salted water and bring to a steady boil. Add spaghetti to vigorously boiling water. Continue to boil pasta until cooked but still al denté, about 10–15 mins.

Drain spaghetti, leaving 1–2 Tbsp of water in pan and return to pan. Keep warm by keeping lid on pan until ready to serve.

Serve spaghetti in individual bowls or in a large central serving dish. Spoon sauce over the top and garnish with chopped parsley and a nondairy parmesan (optional).

*Follow packet instructions for reconstituting TVP.
For Textured Vegetable Protein, see p. 13.*

PER SERVING	Calories 502	Protein 24g	Fat 6g	Carbohydrates 88g	Sugar 9g	Fiber 20g	Sodium 385mg

MOCK CHICKEN LOAF

1 cup whole wheat or buckwheat
(small) pasta, cooked in salted water

1½ Tbsp smooth peanut butter

1 tsp oil

2 onions, finely chopped

1 cup light nondairy milk

2 Tbsp potato starch,
mixed with 6 Tbsp water

1 cup fresh whole wheat/rye
breadcrumbs*

1 tsp stock powder (p. 83)

1 tsp mixed herbs

SERVES 6

Here is one of my mother's favorite dishes. I have replaced the two eggs she used with cornstarch or potato starch.

Preheat oven to 350°F.

Cook pasta according to packet instructions. Drain and place cooked pasta into a bowl and mash well.

Add the remaining ingredients into the hot pasta, starting with peanut butter.

Spoon mixture into a loaf pan (8 × 4 inch) lined with parchment paper. Cover with foil lined with parchment paper and bake in preheated oven for 1–1¼ hr or until loaf is firm to touch.

Cool completely before removing from baking pan.

Garnish with chopped parsley, cherry tomatoes, or carrot curls. Cut into slices and serve.

PER SERVING	Calories 237	Protein 9g	Fat 5g	Carbohydrates 39g	Sugar 5g	Fiber 4g	Sodium 267mg

SPICED RED LENTIL CASSEROLE GF

This is a well tried recipe with a lovely spice related distinctive flavor. You may replace eggplant with two zucchinis if preferred.

Preheat oven to 350°F.

In a bowl cover lentils with hot water, set aside, and allow lentils to soak for 30 mins.

Roast fennel, coriander, and cumin seeds in a hot pan until they become aromatic (2–3 mins). Then in a coffee grinder, grind seeds to powder.

Sauté spices, garlic, and onions (without oil) in a hot saucepan, stirring continuously until onions are translucent and lightly golden. Add 2 Tbsp water if needed to prevent burning.

Add the eggplant, carrots, and potatoes. Stir well ensuring vegetables are coated with the spices.

Now add the tomato paste, chopped tomatoes, and stock. Stir well and allow the mixture to come to a boil. Simmer for 10 mins before adding the drained red lentils. Combine thoroughly.

Spoon into a casserole dish, cover with foil lined with parchment paper and bake in oven for 45 mins. Remove cover after 30 mins and allow the surface of the dish to brown and turn golden.

Garnish with ¼ cup chopped coriander (cilantro).

13 oz red lentils

2 tsp coriander seeds

1 tsp fennel seeds

1 tsp cumin seeds

2 cloves garlic, crushed

2 medium onions, chopped coarsely

1 medium eggplant, coarsely chopped

1½ cups carrot, grated

1 medium-sized potato, cut into ½ inch cubes

2 Tbsp tomato paste

2–3 tomatoes, chopped

3 cups water with 2 ½ tsp stock powder (p. 83)

¼ cup parsley or coriander

SERVES 4

| PER SERVING | Calories 428 | Protein 29g | Fat 3g | Carbohydrates 69g | Sugar 15g | Fiber 16g | Sodium 379mg |

MOCK CHICKEN LOAF (P. 55)

MOUSSAKA

2 generous cups spiral pasta
or macaroni

3–4 large potatoes,
peeled, cooked, and mashed

1 cup of reconstituted TVP mince
(textured vegetable protein)*

2 cloves garlic, crushed

2 medium onions, chopped

2 cups fresh tomatoes, chopped

2 Tbsp tomato paste

2 medium zucchini, chopped

1 medium carrot, chopped

1 cup peas

1½ cups water with 1¼ tsp stock
powder (p. 83)

3 cups of béchamel sauce
(p. 85)

SERVES 8

This is a Greek national dish and was given to me by some of my work colleagues. It is one of many variations and is an ideal dish when entertaining larger groups. Moussaka may be served hot or cold with a salad the next day.

Preheat oven to 350°F. Cook the pasta in plenty of water until al denté, drain, cover, and set aside.

Cook the potatoes and mash them well. Reconstitute TVP (according to packet instructions) and set aside.

Sauté garlic and onions (without oil), stirring to prevent burning. Add 2 Tbsp hot water if needed, and cook until onions are soft and translucent. Add tomatoes, tomato paste, zucchini, carrot, peas, and stock. Combine well.

Add TVP. Mix well and allow to simmer gently for 7–10 mins until vegetables are cooked and liquid has reduced a little. Now add the cooked pasta and combine.

Place mixture in a casserole dish and spoon the mashed potatoes over the top. Smooth the surface of the potato evenly, right to the edges before finally adding the béchamel sauce.

Place casserole dish in the preheated oven for 45 mins. Sprinkle with parsley before serving.

* Follow packet instructions for reconstituting TVP.

PER SERVING   Calories 282   Protein 15g   Fat 6g   Carbohydrates 42g   Sugar 8g   Fiber 8g   Sodium 234mg

CARROT &
ZUCCHINI
TERRINE
(P. 58)

CARROT AND ZUCCHINI TERRINE

This dish looks amazing on a platter with it's layers of mouthwatering colors. Though somewhat time consuming, the finished product is well worth the effort, especially for a special occasion. Try reversing the colors for a change.

Line a loaf pan (10½ × 5 inch) with parchment paper (unless it is nonstick) and preheat oven to 350°F.

Remove stalks from spinach and set spinach aside.

PREPARE THE CARROT LAYER:

Place carrot slices in a double boiler with grated ginger and steam until soft and cooked. Spoon carrots into a bowl and mash them well. Add honey, salt, tomato paste, and dissolved corn/potato starch to mixture. Combine well and set aside to cool.

PREPARE ZUCCHINI LAYER:

Sauté garlic and onion (without oil) in a hot pan adding 2 Tbsp of water as needed to prevent burning, while stirring continually; then add zucchini and mix well. Add stock powder and dried herbs. Cook gently until zucchini is cooked through. Place the zucchini mixture in a bowl and mash, then add breadcrumbs. Remove from heat and set aside to cool before adding the dissolved corn/potato starch and chopped nuts. Combine well and set aside to cool.

TO ASSEMBLE:

Spoon carrot mixture into the base of the loaf pan, pressing down well. Then carefully place the spinach leaves on top, making sure the edges are covered well with the leaves. Finally, spoon in the zucchini mixture, and press down well.

Cover with foil lined with parchment paper and seal. Bake in preheated oven for 1 hr. Allow to cool completely before turning out. Garnish with carrot or zucchini curls, depending on the color of the top layer.

CARROT LAYER:

2 packed cups
baby spinach leaves

6–7 medium carrots, sliced

2 tsp fresh ginger, grated

1 tsp honey

½ tsp salt

2 Tbsp tomato paste

2 Tbsp corn/potato starch,
dissolved in 6 Tbsp water

ZUCCHINI LAYER:

2 cloves garlic, crushed

1 medium onion, chopped

6 cups zucchini, finely chopped

1¼ tsp stock powder (p. 83)

1 generous pinch each dried
basil, oregano, and sage

1 cup whole wheat breadcrumbs

2 Tbsp potato starch,
dissolved in 6 Tbsp water

½ cup almonds or cashews,
finely chopped

SERVES 6

PER SERVING	Calories 302	Protein 16g	Fat 10g	Carbohydrates 37g	Sugar 16g	Fiber 12g	Sodium 467mg

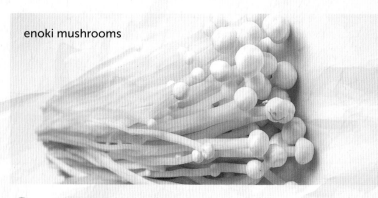

enoki mushrooms

black fungi mushr

PAD THAI NOODLES

15 oz udon or rice noodles

4 Tbsp lime juice

1 cup water with 1 tsp stock powder (p. 83)

2 tsp cornstarch

3 Tbsp light soy sauce

2 tsp oil

1–2 red chiles, finely sliced

4 cloves garlic, chopped

4 oz mixed Asian (black fungi and enoki) mushrooms

7 oz bean sprouts (optional)

5 oz firm or marinated tofu, finely sliced

2 Tbsp coriander leaves, chopped

3 Tbsp roasted peanuts, crushed

¼ cup sliced spring/green onions

SERVES 4

This recipe is a very tasty dish. I used two 3-inch long red chiles for a medium-hot dish. For a mild, use only one chile. I removed the seeds as they add more heat, but this is optional.

Prepare noodles according to packet instructions, cover and set aside.

Place lime juice, stock, cornstarch, and soy sauce together in a small bowl and whisk well. Set aside.

Heat a wok or large heavy-based saucepan until very hot. Then add oil and move the wok around until the oil has coated most of the sides. Add the chopped chiles and garlic and stir well for 2–3 mins or until cooked through.

Add the drained noodles, mushrooms, and bean sprouts and stir gently to mix. Cook for about 2 mins until all ingredients are well mixed through and partly cooked.

Add the lime juice, stock, cornstarch, and soy sauce to the ingredients and gently stir all ingredients together before you bring it back to heat. As a last ingredient add tofu and gently mix through.

To serve, spoon ingredients into warmed serving bowls. Sprinkle with the roasted nuts, coriander leaves, and finally the sliced spring/green onions.

PER SERVING   Calories 530   Protein 17g   Fat 13g   Carbohydrates 86g   Sugar 3g   Fiber 9g   Sodium 657mg

FOR ENOKI AND BLACK FUNGI MUSHROOMS. P. 58

MISO AND TOFU STIR FRY 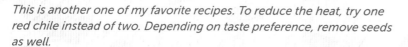 GF

This is another one of my favorite recipes. To reduce the heat, try one red chile instead of two. Depending on taste preference, remove seeds as well.

Prepare miso paste by sautéing garlic and ginger in 1 tsp oil in a wok over a medium-hot heat for a minute. Add miso and sugar stirring in well for about 3 mins until mixture is slightly darkened. Remove and set aside (use 1 Tbsp of this paste in the main recipe).

Add 1 tsp oil to the hot wok and coat the inside. Add the chile, half the spring/green onions, kaffir lime leaves and stir continuously for 1 min.

Add tofu and fry until tofu is slightly charred. Stir in stock, sugar, and bean paste and bring back to a simmer. Then add the bean sprouts, shredded mango, soy sauce, and torn coriander leaves and lime juice. Stir mixture gently and combine well. Remove from heat and serve garnished with spring/green onions.

Remove kaffir lime leaves and serve with rice.

For shredding mango see instructions on p. 37.

MISO PASTE:

1 clove garlic, chopped
2 Tbsp fresh ginger, grated
1 tsp oil
1 Tbsp light miso paste (p. 12)
2 tsp palm sugar

MAIN RECIPE:

1 tsp oil
2 small red chiles, finely sliced
¼ cup spring/green onions, sliced diagonally
5 kaffir lime leaves
15 oz firm tofu, sliced in 1-inch wide rectangles
1 cup water with ½ tsp stock powder (p. 83)
2 tsp palm sugar (optional)
1 Tbsp miso paste (above)
1 cup bean sprouts
1 medium-sized green mango, shredded*
1 Tbsp low salt soy sauce
¼ cup torn coriander leaves, for garnish
juice of 1 lime or lemon
SERVES 4

PER SERVING	Calories 205	Protein 16g	Fat 9g	Carbohydrates 15g	Sugar 14g	Fiber 7g	Sodium 454mg

SPICED PUMPKIN FETTUCCINE WITH LIME (P. 61)

SPICED PUMPKIN FETTUCCINE WITH LIME

12 oz whole-grain or spelt
fettucine

1 tsp oil

2 tsp vegetarian curry paste*

2 tsp palm sugar

2½ cups pumpkin,
peeled and cut into
1 inch cubes

2 lemongrass stalks,
bruised (massaged)

7 oz light coconut milk, diluted
with 3 oz water

1 Tbsp tamarind paste, well
dissolved in ½ cup hot water

juice of 1 lime

2 Tbsp peanuts, toasted

¼ cup coriander, chopped

SERVES 4

The addition of lemongrass adds a rather interesting flavor to the spiciness of this dish. If you prefer less heat then simply adjust the curry paste to your personal taste.

Cook fettucine in boiling water according to instructions. Drain pasta then return to saucepan with 2 Tbsp of the water to prevent fettucine drying out, and cover.

Place oil in another hot pan. Gradually add curry paste and cook for 1 min avoiding the "spitting" from the paste by partially replacing lid while continuing to stir. Add sugar and stir for another minute while cooking.

Add pumpkin and lemongrass and stir for another 2–3 mins until pumpkin is well coated. Next add the coconut milk with water, bring to a boil and simmer very gently for 20 mins or until pumpkin is tender but still firm.

Ten minutes before the pumpkin is cooked, add the tamarind paste and lime juice and stir in well. Remove from heat and take out lemongrass stalks before adding half the peanuts. Keep warm. Prior to serving add sauce to the pasta and using tongs gently toss.

Place pasta into a warmed serving dish, placing a few pieces of reserved pumpkin on top. Garnish with coriander and remaining peanuts.

*Vegetarian curry paste is available from most good supermarkets or health-food stores. If not then ask if they can get it for you.

PER SERVING   Calories 482   Protein 12g Fat 10g Carbohydrates 86g Sugar 15g   Fiber 7g   Sodium 280mg

---

2 cloves garlic, crushed

2 large onions, chopped

½ cup sunflower seeds

1 red pepper, diced

1 Tbsp tamari

1½ cups of water with 1 tsp stock
powder (p. 83)

2 Tbsp tomato paste

2 Tbsp parsley, chopped

2 tsp basil leaves, oregano, and
paprika

2 cups red kidney beans, cooked

1 cup black beans, cooked

2–3 cups potato,
cooked and mashed

SHEPHERD'S PIE

This is Jennifer Beadnell's recipe. Try with sweet potato for a different flavor.

Preheat oven to 350°F.

Sauté garlic, onions, and pepper (without oil), add 2 Tbsp hot water if needed to prevent burning. Add sunflower seeds and sauté for 1–2 mins.

Add pepper, tamari, stock, tomato paste, parsley, and herbs. Stir well and cook gently for 2–3 mins. Add the beans and adjust flavor by adding more herbs as desired.

Spread mixture into a deep pie dish. Top with mashed potatoes.

Place in preheated oven for about 30 mins to brown the top.
Serve warm. **SERVES 6**

PER SERVING   Calories 591   Protein 38g Fat 7g Carbohydrates 94g Sugar 12g   Fiber 18g   Sodium 557mg

THAI CHICKPEA AND CASHEW CURRY (GF)

This is a family favorite that will appeal to those who like spicy Asian food. You may wish to adjust curry paste according to your personal taste or replace curry paste with fresh chile instead.

Add oil to a large hot saucepan. Add the cumin seeds, garlic, and red curry paste and cook for 1 min while stirring. Add the onions and carrots and cook while stirring for 2–3 mins until tender.

Blend in coconut milk and bring to simmer (if more liquid is required use soy milk or stock at the very end of cooking).

Add green beans and reduce heat and simmer for 8–10 mins or until sauce has thickened slightly.

Mix in chickpeas, peas, and remaining ingredients then simmer gently for another 15–20 mins until vegetables are just tender. Add the cashews last and combine.

Serve topped with coriander and accompanied with 4 cups cooked rice.

1 tsp olive oil

1 tsp cumin seeds

2 cloves garlic, crushed

¼ cup red vegetarian curry paste

1 onion, thinly sliced

2 carrots, chopped

5 oz light coconut milk, diluted with 3 oz water

4 oz green beans, trimmed and halved

21 oz cooked chickpeas or 2×15 oz cans chickpeas, well drained and rinsed

1 cup frozen peas

2 Tbsp tamarind paste (p. 13) mixed with ¼ cup water

2 tsp brown sugar

4 Tbsp lime juice (lemons may do if limes are not available)

½ cup chopped coriander

¼ cup toasted cashews (or peanuts if cashews are not available)

SERVES 6

PER SERVING   Calories 308   Protein 14g   Fat 12g   Carbohydrates 36g   Sugar 14g   Fiber 14g   Sodium 278mg

A SPICY THAI DISH WITH CURRY AND TAMARIND PASTE

FALAFEL #1

A staple Middle Eastern dish made with chickpeas (garbanzos). It will surprise you.

1½ cups broad or fava beans (frozen may be used)

2 tsp cumin seeds

2 tsp coriander seeds

2 oz cooked chickpeas

3 Tbsp onions, chopped

2 cloves garlic

½ cup parsley, chopped

¼ cup mint, chopped

¼ cup fresh coriander leaves, chopped

½ tsp salt

2 tsp honey

SERVES 6

Preheat oven to 350°F.

Simmer broad/fava beans in 2 cups of boiling water for 5 mins. Drain and set aside.

Toast cumin and coriander seeds in a hot saucepan for 2–3 mins or until aromatic then grind seeds in a coffee grinder. Place cumin and coriander powder together with all the ingredients, including beans, in a food processor and pulse blend for a few seconds until a coarse mixture is formed.

Using a tablespoon, roll mixture into round balls and refrigerate for about 30 mins. Place these falafel balls onto oven tray lined with parchment paper and bake for 25–30 mins in the oven or until balls are nicely golden.

Makes about 18–20 falafel balls.

PER SERVING	Calories 121	Protein 10g	Fat 1g	Carbohydrates 18g	Sugar 4g	Fiber 6g	Sodium 321mg

FALAFEL #2

This is a quick version utilizing a commercial falafel mix made with chickpea flour and only a few other natural ingredients,

1 cup falafel mix

1 cup mixed vegetables, finely chopped, such as:

carrots

tomatoes

celery

spring/green onion

½ cup of breadcrumbs

SERVES 4

Preheat oven to 350°F.

Make up falafel mix according to packet instructions. Set aside.

Add finely chopped vegetables and mix in well. Finally add enough breadcrumbs to make a firm mixture. Combine well.

Using a tablespoon, roll mixture into round balls (size will depend on how much you put on the spoon). Place balls onto an oven tray lined with parchment paper and bake in the oven for 30 mins or until baked falafels are lightly browned and golden. Remove from oven and serve with hummus or a little sweet chile sauce.

Garnish with freshly chopped coriander.

Makes 10–12 falafel balls.

PER SERVING	Calories 150	Protein 6g	Fat 5g	Carbohydrates 20g	Sugar 4g	Fiber 6	Sodium 300mg

STIR-FRIED VEGETABLES WITH NOODLES

Here is another recipe my family likes. Water chestnuts add a nice crunch to this dish. Try using variations on this recipe such as different vegetables, with or without the chile.

Prepare all ingredients prior to cooking and work quickly when stir-frying so vegetables remain al denté when served.

Prepare noodles according to packet instructions, cover and set aside.

Drop oil into a hot wok then add the garlic, ginger, and chile and stir well for 30 secs. Then add the onion slices, stirring well to prevent burning. Add the beans, carrots, pepper, and white ends of bok choy. Mix well with other ingredients and cook with lid on for about 4–5 mins or until vegetables are cooked but still al denté. Add noodles, water chestnuts, and greens from the bok choy. Stir until all ingredients are well combined.

Place the cornstarch, brown sugar, stock, and soy sauce in a separate bowl. Whisk until all the ingredients are dissolved and add to the vegetables and stir gently, thoroughly combining all ingredients. Once sauce thickens, place into a serving bowl and serve immediately.

Garnish with chopped parsley and sprinkle with toasted sesame seeds.

4 oz rice noodles

2 tsp oil

3 cloves garlic, crushed

½–1 knob fresh ginger, grated

1 small red chile, chopped

2 onions, sliced

3½ oz fresh green beans, sliced, or zucchini, cut into matchsticks

1 carrot, cut into 1½ inch long matchsticks

1 red pepper, chopped

1 bunch bok choy, cut into ½–1 inch chunks including white base

1 small can water chestnuts

2 Tbsp brown sugar

1 tsp cornstarch

1 tsp stock powder (p. 83)

3 Tbsp light soy sauce

1 cup water

2 Tbsp sesame seeds, toasted

SERVES 6

PER SERVING	Calories 255	Protein 8g	Fat 7g	Carbohydrates 40g	Sugar 13g	Fiber 9g	Sodium 349mg

VEGETABLES RETAIN THEIR NUTRITIONAL VALUE WHEN LIGHTLY COOKED.

BLACK BEAN SPAGHETTI WITH RED CURRY SAUCE (GF)

¼ cup each red and yellow peppers, roasted and cut into thin strips

8 oz black bean spaghetti

1 onion, finely chopped

1 Tbsp fresh ginger, grated

2 cloves garlic, chopped

1 Tbsp vegetarian red curry paste

4 oz light coconut milk with 3 Tbsps water added

1 cup baby spinach leaves, stalks removed

GARNISH:

1 Tbsp finely sliced spring/green onion

1 Tbsp finely sliced red onion

¼ cup chopped fresh coriander leaves

SERVES 4

This spaghetti has an interesting texture and is a pleasant change from the commercial brands of spaghetti. Made from black beans, it can be replaced with spaghetti made with other beans as well. But I like the depth of color with this variety, as it forms a nice base to the contrasting bright colors of the vegetables.

Preheat oven to 350°F. Roast pepper in preheated oven for 40 mins until soft or lightly charred. Remove from oven and cover for 15 mins. Remove skins, cut into strips, and set aside.

Cook spaghetti according to packet instructions. When cooked, drain and return to saucepan with 1 Tbsp boiling water. Cover, keep warm and set aside.

Meanwhile sauté onion, ginger, and garlic (without oil) in a hot pan for a few minutes until onions are soft and translucent then add the curry paste. Stir carefully as the curry paste is inclined to "spit." Stir gently over a low heat for a few seconds. Add coconut milk with water and combine well. Turn off heat, add spinach leaves and allow to wilt.

Add pepper strips and spaghetti to sauce. Combine gently. Spoon into a serving bowl. Garnish with sliced green and red onion and finish with the coriander. Serve warm.

TIP: Black bean spaghetti should be available in specialty stores or health-food stores.

PER SERVING	Calories 240	Protein 8g	Fat 4g	Carbohydrates 43g	Sugar 4g	Fiber 4	Sodium 385mg

BLACK BEANS ARE POWER PACKED WITH HIGH PROTEIN AND FIBER.

VEGETABLE CURRY

Desley Waterfield. This is a friend's well-tried curry recipe.

Soak saffron in ¼ cup warm water for 15 mins to infuse.

Toast cumin, coriander seeds, and star anise in a hot saucepan until aromatic (about 2–3 mins). Remove from heat and grind in a coffee grinder. Set aside.

Sauté garlic, onions, and curry paste (without oil) in a medium-hot saucepan for a 30 to 45 seconds until onions are soft, taking care when adding curry paste as it tends to "spit."

Add chopped tomatoes and stir. Then add coconut milk, saffron plus water, stock, ground seeds (spices), and shredded coconut, stirring well and simmer for 2–3 mins.

Add the carrot, leek, zucchini, eggplant, red and green peppers, cardamom powder, lime juice, and verjus. Continue to simmer gently for 20 mins or until vegetables are cooked but still al denté.

Spoon into a serving dish and garnish with chopped coriander. Serve with rice.

*Vegetarian curry paste is available in better health-food stores.

TIP: If preferred use 1–2 green or red fresh deseeded chiles in place of curry paste.

½ tsp saffron, soaked in warm water
2 tsp cumin seeds
1 Tbsp coriander seeds
2 star anise
2 cloves garlic, crushed
1 large onion, chopped
1 Tbsp vegetarian curry paste*
2 tomatoes, chopped
5 oz coconut milk with 3 Tbsp water added
2 Tbsp shredded coconut
1¼ cups water with 1 tsp stock powder (p. 83)
1 medium carrot, diced
1 leek, finely sliced
2 zucchini, cut into ½ inch cubes
1 eggplant, cut into ½ inch cubes
½ green pepper, cut into ½ inch cubes
½ red pepper, cut into ½ inch cubes
1 tsp cardamom powder
juice of ½ lime
3 oz verjus
1 handful coriander, chopped
SERVES 6

star anise   saffron

PER SERVING | Calories 189 | Protein 7g | Fat 9g | Carbohydrates 20g | Sugar 19g | Fiber 13g | Sodium 335

PUMPKIN AND FETA TARTS

Another of Jennifer's recipes.

PASTRY:

1 cup whole wheat or spelt flour

2 Tbsp oil

1 tsp salt

¼ cup water

FILLING:

2 cups pumpkin, cooked

2 cups sweet potato, cooked (orange and white)

2 cloves garlic

¼ cup of dairy-free feta cheese

8 oz pkt silken tofu

¼ cup fresh basil leaves, chopped

1 tsp olive oil

SERVES 6

Preheat oven to 350°F. Mix the oil and salt together, add to flour, then add water. Combine well. Refrigerate for 30 mins. Cut pastry and ease into 6 muffin or loose-bottom flan tins. Bake in preheated oven for 10 mins. Allow to cool and set aside.

Peel pumpkin and sweet potato and place in baking dish with garlic (still in skin). Bake in preheated oven until cooked (about 35 mins).

Remove from oven. When cool, squeeze garlic out of skin and mash. Place all cooked vegetables in a bowl. Add crumbled feta, mashed tofu, and basil. Combine well.

Place filling in pastry bases and bake until golden brown for about 30 mins.

PER SERVING	Calories 297	Protein 10g	Fat 13g	Carbohydrates 35g	Sugar 6g	Fiber 10g	Sodium 387mg

CHICKPEA AND LENTIL PATTIES

I think you will like this recipe.

1 tsp oil

1 Tbsp ground turmeric

1 Tbsp cumin seeds, freshly ground

3 cloves garlic, crushed

2 onions, finely sliced

14 oz cooked chickpeas

14 oz cooked brown lentils (if using canned, drain and rinse well)

½ cup sunflower seeds

2 Tbsp walnuts, chopped

½ cup coriander (plus extra coriander leaves for garnishing)

½ cup besan (chickpea) flour

3 Tbsp cornstarch
mixed with 9 Tbsp water

1 cup whole wheat breadcrumbs for coating

SERVES 4

Drop oil into a hot saucepan and add turmeric and ground cumin. Stir for a few seconds then add garlic and onion and cook over a medium–hot heat for 2–3 mins stirring frequently until onion is soft and transparent.

Place chickpeas, lentils, and sunflower seeds in a food processor and blend for a few seconds until mixture is like coarse breadcrumbs.

Transfer to a bowl and add onions, garlic, spices, sunflower seeds, walnuts, and chopped coriander. Add besan (chickpea) flour and stir until well combined. Add the dissolved cornstarch and combine thoroughly.

Form mixture into 12 to 14 patties and coat with breadcrumbs. Bake in the oven for 30 mins or until lightly golden brown.

Serve with apple chutney (p. 84) or sweet and sour sauce (p. 87) and serve while still warm.

Patties can be stored covered in a refrigerator for up to 3 days.

PER SERVING	Calories 689	Protein 41g	Fat 13g	Carbohydrates 102g	Sugar 8g	Fiber 23g	Sodium 261mg

Sweet Things

While it is not necessary to serve a dessert at the end of a meal, it is nearly always appreciated by family and friends. Here are some sweet offerings for you to try. Obviously, some of these recipes are for special occasions only, so small servings are recommended.

SIMPLY IRRESISTIBLE WHEN BERRIES ARE IN SEASON

"When you sit down to dine with a ruler, note well what is before you. . . . Do not crave his delicacies, for that food is deceptive." PROVERBS 23:1–3, NIV

PASTRY BASE:

1 cup rolled oats, (uncooked)

½ cup walnuts, ground

¾ cup desiccated coconut

6 fresh dates, cover with hot water and let stand for 30 mins

1 tsp guar gum powder (p. 12)

½ tsp vanilla extract

FILLING:

2 tsp agar-agar

2 cups cashew pieces

6 dates (soaked in hot water for 30 mins)

¼ tsp vanilla extract

pinch of salt

½ cup water

¼ cup light coconut milk

2 Tbsp maple syrup

TOPPING:

1 ½ tsp agar-agar

½ cup water

juice of half a lemon

3 cups frozen blueberries

2 scant tsp agar-agar

½ cup water

juice of half a lemon

2 Tbsp maple syrup

SERVES 8

BLUEBERRY CHEESECAKE

Maureen le Fanue

This recipe is made in 3 parts—the base, filling, and topping. Guar gum, holds the pastry base together nicely, however, you can also serve this recipe without the base if you desire to reduce the fat content. Small servings are recommended for this special occasion dessert. For a change try using raspberries in place of blackcurrants for a different color topping.

BASE: Heat oven to 350°F. Blend rolled oats, walnuts, and coconut in a food processor until crumbs are formed. Add soaked dates plus water, guar gum, and vanilla. Blend well. Press mixture into a 13½ × 5 inch rectangular baking pan with a loose base. Bake for 10–15 mins. Let it cool completely before filling, or store in a cool, dry place until ready to fill. The base can be made in advance.

This recipe is enough to cover the sides as well as the base of this sized pan.

FILLING: Prepare agar-agar (p. 10) and set aside to cool slightly. Place remaining ingredients in a food processor and blend until smooth. Warm the blended ingredients to body temperature before adding the cooled agar-agar and whisk in well. Pour mixture over the base and refrigerate for 2–3 hrs until firmly set.

TOPPING: Prepare agar-agar then set aside to cool slightly. Pour water and lemon juice into a medium-sized saucepan and heat gently. Add blueberries and stir gently for about 2–3 mins. Add the slightly cooled agar-agar and whisk in well.

Carefully pour the blueberry topping over the filling and smooth the surface with a spatula.

Cover and refrigerate for at least 4 hrs and serve chilled. Cut into equal sized squares or slices and garnish each with a blackcurrant or raspberry and a small mint leaf.

PER SERVING   Calories 409   Protein 9g   Fat 29g   Carbohydrates 28g   Sugar 17g   Fiber 9g   Sodium 29mg

Variation: Follow recipe as given but place pastry base and filling (without topping) in a round 9 inch spring-form tin and dress surface with blueberries and other seasonal berries (see photo opposite).

STRAWBERRY ICE CREAM MOUSSE GF

This is such an easy and quick dessert that will not sit around for very long.

Put frozen sliced bananas into a sturdy food processor, add enough milk to get the ingredients moving. For a softer consistency, add more milk. Finally add rosewater and blend briefly.

Layer glasses alternating with mousse, sliced strawberries, and blueberries, adding more mousse and finishing with the fruit and mint. Finally sprinkle surface with a crushed biscotti.

Variation: Use blueberries or strawberries for a blue or pink ice cream mousse.

4 ripe bananas, peeled and frozen

1 tsp rosewater

¾-1 cup nondairy milk

8 oz strawberries

4 sprigs mint

3 oz blueberries

4 amaretti biscotti

1 tsp vanilla extract

SERVES 4

PER SERVING	Calories 144	Protein 4g	Fat 4g	Carbohydrates 23g	Sugar 16g	Fiber 3g	Sodium 35mg

ADD STRAWBERRIES FOR A PINK ICE CREAM MOUSSE

CHOCOLATE AND ORANGE TART WITH ORANGE SAUCE (GF)

Here is another special occasion dessert.

PASTRY BASE:

1 cup desiccated coconut
6 dates
soaked in hot water for ½ hr
½ cup ground walnuts
½ cup quick rolled oats
½ tsp vanilla extract
¾ tsp guar gum powder (p. 12)

FILLING:

3 tsp agar-agar powder
2–3 ripe avocados
¼ cup pure maple syrup
2 Tbsp carob or cacao powder
4 Tbsp orange juice
2 tsp grated orange zest
1 tsp vanilla extract
pinch cinnamon
pinch salt
orange zest cut into strips
for garnishing
extra orange juice as needed

ORANGE SAUCE:

1 cup fresh orange juice
1 Tbsp maple syrup
1 tsp grated orange zest

SERVES 6

PASTRY BASE:

Blend all ingredients together with dates and water, until mixture becomes a moist soft ball. Press mixture evenly into the bases and sides of 6 individual flan pans with loose bases. Bake in oven for 10 mins.

Let them cool completely before filling.

FILLING:

Prepare agar powder (p. 10) and set aside to let it cool.

Place avocados, maple syrup, carob/cacao powder, orange juice, orange zest, vanilla, cinnamon, and salt in a processor and blend until very smooth. The mixture may need help for it to blend well. If so, use some additional orange juice.

Gently warm chocolate mixture in a saucepan to body temperature. Then add warm agar-agar and whisk in well. Pour mixture into prepared pastry bases. Refrigerate 1 hr to allow mixture to set.

ORANGE SAUCE:

Mix ingredients together in a saucepan and gently simmer over a low-medium heat (stirring occasionally) for about 15 mins until sauce becomes thick and syrupy. Reducing the sauce further will make the sauce thicker. Serve separately with tarts.

Garnish with orange zest strips, a light sprinkle of cacao powder, and an orange wedge.

PER SERVING	Calories 335	Protein 4g	Fat 27g	Carbohydrates 24g	Sugar 18g	Fiber 6g	Sodium 117mg

CHOCOLATE BAVARIAN CREAM PIE

Myrna Fenn

Without cacao this becomes a white desert. Serve with fresh fruit such as strawberries, blueberries, or peach slices placed decoratively on top. Again, a dessert for special occasions.

PASTRY BASE:

Blend all ingredients together with dates and water until mixture becomes a moist soft ball. Press mixture evenly into the base and sides of a round 10 inch springform pan. Bake at 350°F for 10 mins. Allow to cool completely before filling.

FILLING:

Prepare agar (p. 10) and set aside to cool for about 5 mins.

Place drained cashews in a processor and blend to a smooth paste, adding 1 Tbsp cold water to aid the process.

Add coconut milk, cacao/carob, maple syrup, vanilla, water, and salt to blended cashews and process until smooth. Warm mixture to body temperature then whisk in the warm agar.

Pour chocolate mixture into the prepared pastry base and refrigerate for 1 hr to set well. Top with tofu whipped cream (p. 91) set with agar-agar (p. 10) and dress with fruit.

PASTRY BASE:

½ cup toasted Brazil or hazelnuts

2 cups cornflakes

¾ cup desiccated (fine) coconut

6 dates, soaked in hot water for 30 mins

1 Tbsp oil

¾ tsp guar gum powder (p. 12)

FILLING:

2 tsp agar-agar powder

1 cup raw cashews, soaked in hot water

6 oz coconut milk with 1 oz water

1 Tbsp cacao/carob powder

½ cup maple syrup

¼ tsp salt

1 tsp vanilla extract

¾ cup water

2 tsp agar-agar powder

SERVES 16

PER SERVING	Calories 159	Protein 3g	Fat 11g	Carbohydrates 12g	Sugar 8g	Fiber 2g	Sodium 47mg

DRESS WITH STRAWBERRIES, BLUEBERRIES, PEACH SLICES, OR MANDARIN SEGMENTS

AVOCADO AND LIME PIE

You will enjoy this special recipe—something for special occasions.

PASTRY BASE:

½ cup toasted Brazil or hazelnuts

2 cups cornflakes

¾ cup desiccated (fine) coconut

6 dates, soaked in hot water for 30 mins

1 Tbsp oil

¾ tsp guar gum powder (p. 12)

FILLING:

2 tsp agar-agar powder

3 ripe avocados

1 cup fresh mango

2 bananas

1 cup fresh lime or lemon juice

1½ cup maple syrup

1 tsp vanilla extract

SERVES 16

PASTRY BASE:

Select a biscuit base recipe (p. 81) and press into the base and ½ way up the sides of a 10 inch round springform pan.

FILLING:

Prepare agar-agar (p. 10) and set aside to let it cool for about 5 mins.

Except for agar-agar, place all other ingredients into a processor. Blend well until mixture is very smooth.

Warm avocado mixture to body temperature, then gradually add the cooled agar-agar, whisking until well combined.

Pour mixture into the biscuit base and place in refrigerator for 2–3 hrs before serving.

Dress with a sprinkling of desiccated (fine) coconut and thin slices of lime.

PER SERVING	Calories 212	Protein 2g	Fat 16g	Carbohydrates 15g	Sugar 12g	Fiber 3g	Sodium 12mg

SERVE WITH TOFU WHIPPED CREAM (P. 91)

APPLE AND BERRY CRUMBLE

Jennifer Beadnell's recipe.

Preheat oven to 350°F.

Place peeled and sliced apples in a pan with some water. Add raisins, cloves, and cinnamon. Bring to a simmer and cook gently for 3 mins before adding berries, orange zest, and honey. Bring back to heat until berries are warmed through.

Pour mixture into the bottom of a serving dish that will take oven heat.

CRUMBLE:

Combine oats, nuts, coconut, flour, and sugar in a bowl and add oil. Mix in well. Spoon crumble over the apple and berries and bake for about 35 mins or until golden brown.

2 green cooking apples

¼ cup sultanas (raisins)

½ tsp ground cloves

½ tsp cinnamon (p. 13)

10 oz frozen mixed berries

grated zest of 1 orange

2 Tbsp honey or maple syrup

CRUMBLE:

½ cup quick rolled oats

½ cup desiccated (fine) coconut

½ cup whole wheat flour

¼ cup soft brown sugar

1 Tbsp olive oil

2 Tbsp walnuts, finely chopped

SERVES 6

| PER SERVING | Calories 276 | Protein 4g | Fat 12g | Carbohydrates 38g | Sugar 26g | Fiber 7g | Sodium 7mg |

FOR COLD WINTER EVENINGS SERVE WITH VANILLA CUSTARD (P. 92)

BANANA PUDDING

Maureen le Fanue

8 bananas

¾ cup dates
(softened in hot water for 30 mins)

1 cup dairy-free milk

6 Tbsp polenta

1 Tbsp maple syrup

SERVES 6

Blend all ingredients until smooth. Pour into a casserole dish and bake for 1 hr at 350°F or until well browned and fudgelike.

Serve with vanilla custard (p. 91).

Variation: pour mixture into a precooked pastry base (p. 81). Use a 14×5 inch rectangular flan pan with a loose base to serve as a banana slice. Top with cashew cream cheese (p. 90).

2 SLICES	Calories 161	Protein 3g	Fat 1g	Carbohydrates 35g	Sugar 23g	Fiber 4g	Sodium 23mg

QUINOA CHOCOLATE FUDGE GF

Maureen le Fanue

4 dates,
(soaked in hot water for 30 mins)

2 cups white quinoa, cooked

1 Tbsp coconut, desiccated (fine)

2 tsp vanilla extract

1 Tbsp cacao/carob powder

1½ Tbsp maple syrup

1 Tbsp peanut butter

½ Tbsp oil

4 strawberries

SERVES 8

Drain dates and place with all other ingredients, except strawberries, in a processor. Blend for 3 mins until mixture is smooth.

Place mixture in a shallow nonstick tray and level the top of the mixture with a knife. Cut into 8 squares and freeze overnight.

Garnish each square with half a fanned strawberry (or a raspberry).

PER SERVING	Calories 206	Protein 7g	Fat 6g	Carbohydrates 31g	Sugar 7g	Fiber 4g	Sodium 5mg

LOVELY FOR AN AFTER DINNER TREAT

Fruit Cakes & Rolls

DIVIDE INTO MUFFIN MOLDS FOR INDIVIDUAL SERVINGS

"Re-educate your sweet tooth to enjoy less concentrated sweets."
DR. H. DIEHL, DHSc

FRUIT CAKE

2 lbs dried mixed fruit

1¼ cup fresh orange juice,

¾ cup water

½ cup chopped walnuts, hazelnuts, or almonds

1 cup self-rising whole wheat flour

1 cup unbleached self-rising plain flour

¼ cup almond meal

1 tsp rosewater (p. 13)

1 tsp orange flower water (p. 22)

whole almonds for garnishing (optional)

SERVES 14
(2 slices per serving)

Delicious! For a special occasion.

Preheat oven to 325°F. Line a 9 inch square cake pan with parchment paper.

Soak the dried fruit in the orange juice and water overnight.

In the morning add the chopped nuts, flour, almond meal, rosewater, and orange flower water. Mix in well.

Spoon mixture into the cake pan and smooth the surface. If using whole almonds, arrange evenly on top.

Place in oven and bake for 1½ hrs or until skewer comes out clean.

Allow to cool in oven. Wrap cake in towels until it is cooled completely to keep cake moist. Store in an airtight container at room temperature.

TIP: This cake can also be divided into muffin tins and cooked at 340°F for 20–25 mins or until cooked, then frozen when cooled.

PER SERVING	Calories 329	Protein 5g	Fat 5g	Carbohydrates 66g	Sugar 51g	Fiber 7g	Sodium 122mg

GINGER AND MACADAMIA CAKE

1½ cups flour
(½ whole wheat spelt, ½ plain)

2 heaped tsp baking powder

¼ tsp salt

¼ cup carob/cacao powder

½ tsp cardamom powder

2 tsp coriander powder

2 Tbsp nondairy milk

½ cup fresh pineapple juice

½ cup dates
(softened in hot water for 30 mins)

¼ cup maple syrup

1 tsp vanilla extract

2 tsp oil

½ cup macadamias, finely chopped

1 Tbsp crystallized ginger, finely chopped

½ cup desiccated (fine) coconut

1 cup grated apple

1 Tbsp macadamia nuts, chopped

SERVES 16

Greg Heywood

This recipe was given to me by a vegan chef. It is a lovely cake.

Preheat oven to 325°F. Prepare a 9 inch round cake pan lined with parchment paper.

In a large mixing bowl (#1) sift together the flour, baking powder, cacao/carob, and ground spices. In a separate bowl (#2) mix together the milk, pineapple juice, dates (with water), maple syrup, vanilla, and oil.

Add the wet ingredients from bowl #2 to dry ingredients from bowl #1 in batches and combine well with a wooden spoon until they are thoroughly mixed. Now fold in the macadamias, ginger, coconut, and apple.

Spoon mixture into prepared cake pan and bake for 45 mins. Remove cake, wrap in towels (to keep moist) and allow to cool.

When completely cool, cover with cashew cream cheese topping (p. 90), garnished with a few finely chopped macadamia nuts.

1 SLICE	Calories 162	Protein 4g	Fat 6g	Carbohydrates 23g	Sugar 11g	Fiber 3g	Sodium 195mg

FRUIT MEDLEY CAKE

Robin Entermann

Here is yet another proven cake recipe. Use for special occasions.

Preheat oven to 350°F.

Soak fruit overnight in 1 cup milk. In the morning, mix all the ingredients together, including the remaining milk to create a soft consistency, stirring well.

Spoon into an 8 inch cake pan lined with parchment paper. Bake for 45 mins. Allow to cool completely before turning out.

15 oz dried fruit mix

3 cups nondairy milk

1 cup self-rising whole wheat flour

1 cup desiccated (fine) coconut

1 Tbsp honey

1 green apple,
peeled and diced

SERVES 12

PER SERVING	Calories 230	Protein 4g	Fat 6g	Carbohydrates 40g	Sugar 30g	Fiber 5g	Sodium 139mg

FRUIT AND NUT ROLL

Margaret Lyon

Combine nuts and seeds with drained soaked dates and blend briefly to obtain a coarse mixture. Divide and roll each half to make 2 thick sausagelike rolls.

Wrap each "sausage" tightly in plastic wrap and refrigerate for a few hours, then slice before serving. If mixture is too dry, moisten with a little orange juice.

Each roll makes 6 thin slices.

17 oz of mixed raw nuts,
finely chopped

1 oz mixed
(sesame and sunflower) seeds

8 oz fresh dates (soaked
in hot water for 30 mins)

SERVES 12

PER SERVING	Calories 127	Protein 2g	Fat 11g	Carbohydrates 5g	Sugar 3g	Fiber 2g	Sodium 2mg

GINGER AND MACADAMIA CAKE (P. 77)

FRUIT BALLS

Robyn Denes

5 Weetabix

¾ cup desiccated (fine) coconut

1½ Tbsp carob powder

¼ cup sultanas (raisins)

¼ cup dried apricots, chopped

¾ cup coconut cream

6 dates (soaked in water for 30 mins)

1 Tbsp honey

1 tsp vanilla extract

Makes 10 balls.

SERVES 10

Crumble Weetabix and mix all dry ingredients. Then combine honey, coconut milk, dates (with water), vanilla and add to dry ingredients. Mix well.

Roll into balls and roll into extra coconut or sifted carob/cacao powder as desired. Store refrigerated.

PER SERVING	Calories 127	Protein 2g	Fat 11g	Carbohydrates 5g	Sugar 3g	Fiber 2g	Sodium 2mg

DATE AND PISTACHIO ROLLS

Robyn Denes

5 Weetabix

1/4 cup desiccated (fine) coconut

3/4 cup pistachio nuts

12 Tbsp rosewater

1 Tbsp honey

5 dates
(soaked in water for 30 mins)

2 Tbsp extra coconut or
cacao/carob for rolling

MAKES 10 BALLS

The rosewater in this recipe adds a surprisingly delicate flavor to the sweetness of the dates.

Crumble Weetabix and place in a blender with dry ingredients first and blend lightly. Add dates with water, then add rosewater and honey. Process gradually until you have a moist mixture that will hold together when rolling. The mixture should be like coarse breadcrumbs when blended.

Roll small tablespoons of mixture into balls and coat with desiccated (fine) coconut, cacao/carob or half and half. Refrigerate before serving.

PER SERVING: 1	Calories 162	Protein 3g	Fat 8g	Carbohydrates 15g	Sugar 10g	Fiber 3g	Sodium 22mg

Pastry Crusts

COCONUT CRUMB CRUST

Blend oatmeal, walnuts, cornflakes, and fine coconut in a food processor until crumbs are formed. Add soaked dates plus water, oil, vanilla, and guar gum and blend well. Press mixture into the bottom of a pie dish or rectangular flan pan.*

Bake at 350°F for 10–15 mins until lightly browned. Allow to cool before adding filling.

*TIP: This recipe is enough for the bottom and sides of a 9 inch pie pan or a 14 × 4 inch rectangular flan pan with loose base.

½ cup rolled oats

1 cup Brazil or hazelnuts, toasted

2 cups cornflakes

¾ cup desiccated (fine) coconut

6 fresh dates,
(softened with hot water for 30 mins)

1 Tbsp oil

¾ tsp guar gum powder (p. 12)

SERVES 16

PER SERVING	Calories 142	Protein 7g	Fat 10g	Carbohydrates 6g	Sugar 3g	Fiber 2g	Sodium 12mg

"Limit the eating of nuts. they are 80% fat and make weight-loss difficult." N. BARNARD, MD

SWEET BISCUIT CRUST GF

½ cup rolled oats

½ cup ground walnuts

1 cup desiccated (fine) coconut

6 fresh dates, (softened in hot water for 30 mins)

½ tsp vanilla extract

¾ tsp guar gum powder (p. 12)

SERVES 1

Sarah Russell

Enjoy this base for your favorite sweet filling.

Blend nuts until crumbs, then add cornflakes, coconut, dates with water, and oil until mixture becomes a moist soft ball. Press mixture evenly into the bottom and sides of an 8 inch springform pan. Bake at 350°F for 10 mins. Allow to cool completely before filling.

Crust may also be stored in an airtight container in a cool dry place until ready to fill for up to 3 days.

Tip: This recipe is enough to cover most of the sides as well as the bottom of this size baking pan.

PER SERVING	Calories 97	Protein 2g	Fat 5g	Carbohydrates 11g	Sugar 1g	Fiber 2g	Sodium 139mg

SAVORY PASTRY CRUST

1 cup whole wheat or spelt flour

2 Tbsp olive oil

1 tsp salt

¼ cup water

SERVES 8

This is a nice pastry crust for savory dishes. This quantity is for the bottom and sides of a rectangular flan pan with a loose base only. If you want to cover the pie, then double the quantity.

Blend together flour and salt then add oil. Add water and combine well. Refrigerate for 30 mins before pressing into an 8 inch diameter baking dish.

Bake in a preheated oven at 350°F for 10 mins. Allow to cool.

PER SERVING	Calories 97	Protein 2g	Fat 5g	Carbohydrates 11g	Sugar 1g	Fiber 2g	Sodium 139mg

A NICE PASTRY CRUST FOR SAVORY PIES

Extras

LEBANESE CRISPS

An excellent alternative to commercial crackers.

Tear the flat bread into 1–2 inch pieces or wedges. Place them onto a baking tray lined with parchment paper. Bake at 325°F for about 10 mins then turn pieces over to brown or crisp the other side.

May be stored in an airtight container for up to 7 days.

6 Lebanese whole wheat flatbreads

SERVES 6

PER SERVING	Calories 157	Protein 6g	Fat 1g	Carbohydrates 31g	Sugar 2g	Fiber 4g	Sodium 184mg

"Commercial brands cannot compare with sauces, dressings, and condiments that are homemade."

"A man too busy to take care of his health is like a mechanic too busy to take care of his tools." SPANISH PROVERB

VEGETABLE STOCK CONCENTRATE

1 medium onion, chopped

1 leek, chopped

3 small-medium carrots, chopped

½ medium sweet potato, chopped (orange variety)

2 celery stalks, chopped

3 shiitake mushrooms

small bunch parsley stems, chopped

3 fresh button mushrooms

1 bay leaf

1 inch piece of kombu sea vegetable (p. 12)

a few fresh leaves of basil, sage, thyme, and rosemary

2 Tbsp salt

3 cups water

Homemade vegetable stock is the best way to obtain stock. It is nutritionally and taste-wise far superior to the commercial powdered varieties.

Place ingredients in a saucepan with cold water and bring to a simmer. Cover with a tight fitting lid and simmer gently for about 1 hr. Remove kombu sea vegetable.

For a clear stock: strain ingredients through a fine sieve or two cheesecloths placed in a strainer with the grain criss-crossing.

For a thick stock: blend the cooked vegetables and liquid in a processor until mixture is very smooth.

Store covered, either in the refrigerator or pour into ice cube containers and freeze. 1 Tbsp of concentrate equates to 1 stock cube or 1 tsp stock powder. This stock can now be used for all your stock requirements.

Makes approximately 50 Tbsp.

1 Tbsp per serving.

TIP: When making vegetable stock avoid using vegetables from the cruciferous family such as broccoli, cabbage, and cauliflower, as they tend to overpower the taste. The addition of shiitaki mushrooms adds flavor while kombu sea vegetable adds desirable nutrients. The salt used in this recipe is designed as a preservative. Less salt will reduce the shelf life accordingly, unless it is frozen.

PER SERVING	Calories 19	Protein 1g	Fat 1g	Carbohydrates 2g	Sugar 1g	Fiber 1g	Sodium 363mg

VEGETABLE SEASONING

2 Tbsp salt

½ cup nutritional yeast flakes

½ tsp turmeric powder

1 tsp garlic powder

1 Tbsp onion powder

½ tsp marjoram, dried

½ tsp sage, dried

1 Tbsp parsley

1 tsp celery seeds

Jean Gidley Ward

Blend ingredients thoroughly to a powderlike consistency. Store in a sealed container in the refrigerator or in a cool dry place. This can be used in place of commercial stock powders.

Makes approximately 25 tsp.

TIP: If using commercial stock powder, use a vegetable based brand (like Massell), but select a low salt variety for reduced salt content.

PER TSP	Calories 15	Protein 2g	Fat 1g	Carbohydrates 1g	Sugar 1g	Fiber 1g	Sodium 713mg

Condiments

APPLE CHUTNEY GF

A happy discovery made during one of my chutney experiments.

Sauté onion in a medium-sized pan until translucent. Add apple and remaining ingredients and return to heat. Simmer gently for 20 mins until mixture turns golden brown, thickens slightly, and most of the liquid has been absorbed. Store refrigerated in a sealed clean jar. Makes about 1½ cups

1 onion, finely chopped
1 green apple, cored, peeled, and diced
2 tsp brown sugar or honey
3 Tbsp currants
¼ cup apple cider vinegar
SERVES 6

	Calories 29	Protein 1g	Fat 1g	Carbohydrates 4g	Sugar 4g	Fiber 1g	Sodium 2mg

APRICOT CHUTNEY GF

Sauté garlic and ginger in a pan over moderate heat until translucent, stirring constantly. Add mustard seeds; sauté for 1 minute, or until fragrant. Add remaining ingredients and simmer gently for 20 mins or until most liquid has been absorbed. Set aside to cool. Store refrigerated.

Makes 1½ cups.

1 tsp ginger, finely chopped
2 cloves garlic, crushed
½ tsp mustard seeds
¾ cup dried apricots, chopped
2 Tbsp currants
½ cup water
2 Tbsp apple cider vinegar
1½ Tbsp brown sugar
1 pinch salt
SERVES 6

	Calories 89	Protein 1g	Fat 1g	Carbohydrates 19g	Sugar 18g	Fiber 3g	Sodium 197mg

DUKKAH GF

This is very tasty and spicy African and Egyptian condiment for sprinkling on salads, wraps, or sandwiches. I've even added dukkah to potatoes before roasting for a lovely spicy flavor.

Dry roast the sesame, nuts, cumin, coriander, fennel, and sunflower seeds in a hot saucepan until aromatic (about 3–5 mins). Shake pan from time to time to prevent seeds from burning. Remove from the pan and allow to cool.

When ingredients have cooled add salt, peppercorns, and dried mint/thyme. Place in a coffee grinder and pulse (turning grinder off and on) every couple of seconds to form a very coarse mix.

Refrigerate in an airtight container to keep fresh until ready to use. Makes about 1 cup.

5 oz sesame seeds
3 Tbsp cumin seeds
4 Tbsp coriander seeds
1 tsp salt
2 Tbsp fennel seeds
1 Tbsp sunflower seeds
½ tsp black peppercorns
1 tsp dried mint or thyme (optional)
3 oz hazelnuts or almonds (or mixture of both)

PER 2 TSP	Calories 123	Protein 8g	Fat 17g	Carbohydrates 7g	Sugar 1g	Fiber 4g	Sodium 154mg

Sauces

BÉCHAMEL SAUCE GF

¼ cup cashews,
soaked in hot water for 30 mins

1 clove garlic, crushed

1 Tbsp nutritional yeast flakes

1 tsp lemon juice

2 tsp potato starch or cornstarch,
mixed with 2 Tbsp cold water

½ tsp onion flakes

1¾ cups water with 1½ tsp stock
powder (p. 83)

freshly ground black
peppercorns to taste

SERVES 4

This sauce is very versatile. Works well with lasagne and other pasta dishes.

Drain cashews and set aside. Place garlic and cashews in a small blender and blend until paste. Add yeast flakes, lemon juice, potato starch or cornstarch, onion flakes, and a little of the stock to the blender and blend well. Add the remaining stock slowly and blend for a few more seconds.

Pour into a saucepan and bring to simmer while stirring continuously until mixture starts to thicken. Add low fat dairy-free milk or additional water if desired for the consistency required. Add a few grinds of salt and a little freshly ground black peppercorns. Do not boil.

Serve with vegetables. Makes about 1½ cups.

PER SERVING	Calories 60	Protein 3g	Fat 4g	Carbohydrates 3g	Sugar 1g	Fiber 1g	Sodium 196mg

ONION SAUCE GF

¼ cup raw cashews
(soaked in hot water for 30 mins)

1 Tbsp yeast flakes

2 tsp lemon juice

2 tsp potato starch or cornstarch,
mixed with 2 Tbsp cold water

½ cup water, with ½ tsp stock
powder (p. 83)

1¼ cup light nondairy milk

1 medium onion, finely chopped

SERVES 4

Soak cashews in hot water for 30 mins then drain and blend well in a processor with a tsp or two of water until cashews resemble a smooth paste (about 2 mins).

Add the other ingredients except onion and milk and blend until mixture is very smooth. Then add milk and blend again for a few seconds.

Sauté onion (without oil) in a hot saucepan for 2–3 mins stirring continuously to prevent burning until onions are translucent and golden. Add a little water as needed. Add onion to the sauce and bring to a gentle simmer, stirring continuously until sauce has thickened.

Serve with vegetables. Makes about 1½ cups.

PER SERVING	Calories 104	Protein 6g	Fat 5g	Carbohydrates 8g	Sugar 3g	Fiber 3g	Sodium 110mg

ROASTED RED PEPPER SAUCE GF

Maureen le Fanue

This is a lovely mildly sweet sauce to be used with your choice of patties. You won't be disappointed.

Bake peppers and garlic (in their skins) on high heat for 30–40 mins. Set aside in a covered bowl to sweat, then remove their skins.

Place peppers and peeled garlic in a processor with all other ingredients and blend for 1–2 mins until mixture is well blended and very smooth. More lemon juice may be added to give a tarter taste. This sauce looks very colorful on the plate.

Refrigerated, it will last for 3–4 days. Makes about 2½ cups.

4–5 medium-sized red peppers

3 baked cloves garlic

2 Tbsp fresh lemon juice

¼ cup light coconut milk

¼ tsp salt

1 pinch ground black peppercorns

SERVES 8

PER SERVING	Calories 49	Protein 3g	Fat 1g	Carbohydrates 7g	Sugar 6g	Fiber 3g	Sodium 74mg

APPLE AND PEANUT SATAY SAUCE GF

Choose unsalted and hulled peanuts for this recipe. Serve with some of the Asian dishes in this book.

Roast peanuts at 280°F for 10 mins. Remove from oven and set aside to cool.

Blend all ingredients in a blender until smooth.

Refrigerate.

Makes about 1½ cups.

1½ cups chopped and peeled Granny Smith apple

1 level tsp chopped ginger

1 cup raw peanuts

1 small red chile

1 tsp lime juice

⅓ cup light coconut milk

1 tsp lemon juice

¼ tsp salt

1 tsp tamari or low salt soy sauce

SERVES 6

PER SERVING	Calories 169	Protein 7g	Fat 13g	Carbohydrates 6g	Sugar 5g	Fiber 3g	Sodium 59mg

APPLE SAUCE GF

This is a lovely mildly sweet sauce that is another nice accompaniment to some of the main dishes in this book.

Core the apples (leave peel on) and cut into 1 inch segments. Place apples in a saucepan, add water, and cook until apples are soft and tender, about 10–15 mins. Add to a blender and process until apples are well blended and smooth.

Makes 1½ cups.

4 large sweet eating apples

⅓ cup orange juice

½ cup water

SERVES 6

PER SERVING	Calories 81	Protein 1g	Fat 1g	Carbohydrates 17g	Sugar 17g	Fiber 4g	Sodium 1mg

SWEET AND SOUR DIPPING SAUCE

¾ cup tomato juice

½ cup unsweetened pineapple juice

1 Tbsp light soy sauce or tamari

2 tsp dark balsamic vinegar

SERVES 6

Try this lovely dipping sauce with Asian spring rolls.

Place all ingredients in a saucepan and simmer uncovered, stirring occasionally until slightly thickened (about 5 mins).

Makes about 1 cup.

PER SERVING	Calories 29	Protein 1g	Fat 1g	Carbohydrates 4g	Sugar 4g	Fiber 1g	Sodium 176mg

BASIL PESTO

4 packed cups basil leaves

1 tsp light soy sauce

1 clove garlic

1 Tbsp water

¼ cup pine nuts
(roasted at 250°F for 8–10 mins)

1 Tbsp lemon juice

2 tsp olive oil

1 pinch salt

SERVES 8

This is my favorite pesto, much lower in oil than those commercial brands.

Place all ingredients except water in a blender and blend until smooth. Add some water to get the blades moving and until desired consistency is obtained.

Place pesto in a bowl and cover surface of pesto with plastic wrap. This prevents pesto surface from discoloring or oxidizing.

Refrigerated, it will keep for up to 1 week.

Makes 1¼ cups

PER SERVING	Calories 57	Protein 2g	Fat 5g	Carbohydrates 1g	Sugar 1g	Fiber 2g	Sodium 45mg

"BASIL AND TOMATOES. A MATCH MADE IN HEAVEN."

Dressings and Mayonnaise

Try selecting a mayonnaise or dressing that provides taste and makes your salad or dish appetizing and still keeps the fat content low.

BASIC VINAIGRETTE

Place ingredients in a screw top jar and shake well or blend with a stick blender.

Serve separately in a small bowl. Makes ⅓ cup.

¼ cup lemon juice
2 tsp olive oil
1 clove garlic, crushed
pinch of salt
1 tsp brown sugar
SERVES 6

PER SERVING	Calories 26	Protein 1g	Fat 2g	Carbohydrates 1g	Sugar 1g	Fiber 1g	Sodium 25mg

CITRUS VINAIGRETTE GF

Place all ingredients in a screw top jar and shake vigorously for 30 secs until well combined.

Serve with salads.

Makes ¾ cup.

½ cup orange juice
3 Tbsp lemon juice
2 tsp balsamic vinegar
1 crushed clove garlic
2 tsp oil
SERVES 6

PER SERVING	Calories 30	Protein 1g	Fat 2g	Carbohydrates 2g	Sugar 2g	Fiber 1g	Sodium 5mg

TOFU MAYONNAISE

Graham Roberts

Place all ingredients in a blender and process until smooth and creamy (about 5 mins). Serve chilled.

Refrigerated, it will keep up to 1 week.

Makes about 1½ cups.

10 oz silken tofu
1 pinch salt
1½ Tbsp lemon juice
½ tsp dijon mustard
1 tsp honey
freshly ground
black pepper to taste
SERVES 4–6

PER SERVING	Calories 38	Protein 3g	Fat 2g	Carbohydrates 3g	Sugar 1g	Fiber 1g	Sodium 37mg

TOFU SOUR CREAM

8 oz silken tofu
2 tsp Dijon mustard
pinch of salt
2 Tbsp lemon juice
1 Tbsp olive oil
SERVES 4

Place all ingredients into a blender and process until smooth and creamy (about 5 mins).

Refrigerate for 1 hr before serving. Will keep for up to a week when stored covered in the refrigerator.

Makes about 1¼ cups

PER SERVING	Calories 74	Protein 4g	Fat 6g	Carbohydrates 1g	Sugar 1g	Fiber 2g	Sodium 98mg

CREAMY TOFU DRESSING

10 oz silken tofu
¼ tsp garlic powder
or 1 small clove of garlic
2 Tbsp lemon juice
¼ tsp salt
2 tsp honey
1 pinch ground black peppercorns
1 tsp prepared horseradish
SERVES 6

Place all ingredients in a blender and process until smooth. Adjust the consistency to your liking by adding small amounts of water or nondairy milk. Chill at least 2 hrs before serving.

Refrigerated, it will keep up to a week.

PER SERVING	Calories 42	Protein 3g	Fat 2g	Carbohydrates 3g	Sugar 2g	Fiber 1g	Sodium 28mg

CAPER ROSEMARY OIL GF

1 Tbsp finely chopped caperberries (p. 12)

2 Tbsp olive oil

1 Tbsp verjus (p. 13)

2 tsp finely chopped rosemary

SERVES 6

This dressing is very nice if served with the purees on p. 44. Although there seems to be a lot of oil in this dressing, only very small amounts are required. Caperberries are obtained from the deli section of good supermarkets.

Chop the berries and combine with the other ingredients. Place in a small saucepan and heat while stirring on a low setting for several minutes.

Makes about ¼ cup.

1 TSP	Calories 53	Protein 1g	Fat 5g	Carbohydrates 1g	Sugar 1g	Fiber 1g	Sodium 49mg

Fruit Sauces, Whipped Cream, and Custard

Select from the puree, custard, or one of the creams, to make your dish appetizing and appealing, yet still keep the fat content low.

CASHEW CREAM CHEESE TOPPING

Drain cashews and place in a processor and blend until cashews form a smooth paste (some water may be added to free the blades).

Add oil, milk, vinegar, lemon juice, salt, syrup, and guar gum. Process for several seconds until mixture is smooth and soft.

Spoon into a bowl and refrigerate for an hour. A little more milk may be added to obtain reasonably firm but soft consistency. Makes about 1¼ cups.

This quantity is enough to cover the 12 serving Ginger and Macadamia Cake (p. 77).

½ cup cashews (soaked in hot water for 30 mins)

1 Tbsp olive oil

1 tsp apple cider vinegar

1 tsp lemon juice

1 pinch salt

2 tsp maple syrup

1 tsp guar gum

¼ cup dairy-free milk

1 tsp vanilla extract

1–2 Tbsp chopped nuts

PER SERVING	Calories 52	Protein 1g	Fat 4g	Carbohydrates 3g	Sugar 1g	Fiber 1g	Sodium 16mg

CASHEW AND SOY CREAM

Myrna Fenn

I first tried this at Myrna's place. Here is her recipe.

Blend the drained cashews and 1 Tbsp nondairy milk well until a smooth paste is formed. Gradually add the rest of the milk, extracts, and maple syrup, until smooth and creamy. You may need to scrape the sides of the blender several times during processing. Refrigerate 1 hr prior to serving. Makes 3 cups. Serves 8.

TIP: Almond extract is more difficult to find but is a far superior product to almond essence.

For a consistency similar to whipped cream, add milk a little at a time to the cashews until the desired consistency is obtained.

1 cup raw cashews, soaked in hot water for 30 mins

2 cups nondairy milk

1 tsp vanilla extract

½ tsp almond extract

½ tsp maple syrup

PER SERVING	Calories 116	Protein 4g	Fat 8g	Carbohydrates 7g	Sugar 3g	Fiber 1g	Sodium 36mg

TOFU WHIPPED CREAM GF

8 oz silken tofu

2 tsp olive oil

1 Tbsp honey or maple syrup

½ tsp lemon juice

1 pinch salt

SERVES 6

Place all ingredients in a blender and blend for 4–5 mins until mixture is increased in volume and becomes "frothy" like whipped cream. Refrigerate for at least 1 hr before serving.

Makes about 1¼ cups.

PER SERVING	Calories 57	Protein 2g	Fat 3g	Carbohydrates 3g	Sugar 3g	Fiber 1g	Sodium 27mg

CASHEW CREAM #1 GF

1¼ cups cashews, soaked for 30 mins in hot water

¾ cup nondairy milk

1 tsp maple syrup

SERVES 6

Grind drained cashews in a blender until paste is formed (a little of the milk can be added to turn nuts into paste).

Mix syrup and dairy-free milk well until combined. Add the liquid to the cashew paste and blend on high for 3–4 mins or until the mixture becomes "frothy" and creamy.

Refrigerate for 1 hr before serving.

Serve with fruit or dessert. Makes about 1½ cups.

PER SERVING	Calories 169	Protein 5g	Fat 13g	Carbohydrates 8g	Sugar 3g	Fiber 2g	Sodium 20mg

CASHEW CREAM #2 GF

1 cup cashews (soaked in hot water for 30 mins)

6 dates, chopped (soaked in hot water for 30 mins)

2 Tbsp water

1 tsp vanilla extract

1 pinch salt

SERVES 6

This is another healthy cream alternative in place of dairy whipped cream.

Place drained cashews in a blender and process well with 1–2 Tbsp of water until a smooth paste is formed. You may need to scrape sides of blender a couple of times during processing.

Add the other ingredients and blend for a couple of minutes.

Refrigerate for 1 hr before serving as the cream thickens on standing.

Refrigerated, it will keep up to a week.

Makes about 1½ cups.

PER SERVING	Calories 134	Protein 3g	Fat 10g	Carbohydrates 8g	Sugar 5g	Fiber 2g	Sodium 28mg

VANILLA CUSTARD (GF)

Margaret Lyon

Place all ingredients in a blender with only 1 cup of milk. Blend for 1 min, add remaining 3 cups of milk, and blend briefly once more. Pour mixture into a saucepan and bring to heat and simmer very gently, stirring constantly, until mixture starts to thicken.

More cornstarch gives a mousse consistency while less gives a custard consistency.

TIP: For a chocolate custard add 1½ Tbsp cacao/carob powder.

4¼ cups nondairy milk
4 tsp cornstarch
1 tsp vanilla extract
½ cup honey or maple syrup
½ cup light coconut milk
SERVES 4

PER SERVING	Calories 176	Protein 4g	Fat 4g	Carbohydrates 31g	Sugar 25g	Fiber 2g	Sodium 73mg

APRICOT PURÉE (GF)

Graham Roberts

This is a tasty purée when served with fresh fruit. Place purée in a small-medium bowl in the center of the platter surrounded by fruit. The addition of this colorful dish is a nice touch.

Put diced apricots and juice into a saucepan and simmer gently for 15 mins until apricots have thickened.

Strain any excess juice then blend apricots with a stick blender or similar until very smooth. Add reserved or additional apple juice to obtain the desired consistency.

Chill until serving time.

Makes about 1½ cups.

1½ cups apricots, chopped
1 cup fresh apple juice
SERVES 6

PER SERVING	Calories 93	Protein 2g	Fat 1g	Carbohydrates 19g	Sugar 18g	Fiber 3g	Sodium 18mg

(93)

Conversion Table Guide

These tables are a guide in the conversion of Metric to Imperial measurements.
For the sake of keeping things simple, I have slightly rounded off the measurements stated below.
All conversions should be sufficiently accurate for all recipes.

ABBREVIATIONS

g	grams
kg	kilograms
oz	ounces
fl oz	fluid ounces
lb	pounds
l	liter
ml	milliliter
mm	millimeter
tsp	teaspoon
Tbsp	tablespoon
pt	pint
qt	quart
gal	gallon

METRIC, CUP & SPOON MEASUREMENTS

*Australian tablespoon is 20 ml, UK is 15 ml, and American is 16 ml.

metric	cup	metric	spoon
60 ml	¼ cup	1¼ ml	¼ teaspoon
80 ml	⅓ cup	2½ ml	½ teaspoon
125 ml	½ cup	5 ml	1 teaspoon
250 ml	1 cup	20 ml*	1 tablespoon

WEIGHT MEASUREMENTS

metric	imperial	pounds	metric	imperial	pounds
10 g	¼ oz		315 g	10 oz	
15 g	½ oz		345 g	11 oz	
30 g	1 oz		375 g	12 oz	¾ lb
60 g	2 oz		410 g	13 oz	
90 g	3 oz		440 g	14 oz	
125 g	4 oz	¼ lb	470 g	15 oz	
155 g	5 oz		500 g	16 oz	1 lb
185 g	6 oz		750 g	24 oz	1½ lb
220 g	7 oz		1 kg	32 oz	2 lb
250 g	8 oz	½ lb	1½ kg	48 oz	3 lb
280 g	9 oz		2 kg	64 oz	4 lb

LIQUID MEASUREMENTS

metric	imperial	cup	metric	imperial	cup
30 ml	1 fl oz		250 ml	8 ¾ fl oz	1 cup
60 ml	2 fl oz	¼ cup	375 ml	13 fl oz	1½ cups
80 ml	3 ½ fl oz	⅓ cup	430 ml	15 fl oz	1 ¾ cups
100 ml	2 ¾ fl oz		500 ml	17 fl oz	2 cups
125 ml	4 fl oz	½ cup	750 ml	26 fl oz	3 cups
150 ml	5 fl oz		1 l	35 fl oz	4 cups
180 ml	6 fl oz	¾ cup	1¼ l	44 fl oz	5 cups
200 ml	7 fl oz		2 l	70 fl oz	8 cups

OVEN TEMPERATURES

Celsius (electric)	Celsius (fan forced)	Fahrenheit	gas	
120°	100°	250°	1	very slow
150°	130°	300°	2	slow
160°	140°	325°	3	moderately slow
180°	160°	350°	4	moderate
190°	170°	375°	5	moderately hot
200°	180°	400°	6	hot
230°	210°	450°	7	very hot
250°	230°	500°	9	very hot

If using a fan-forced oven, your cooking time may be a little quicker, so start checking your food a little sooner.
Reference: www.measurement.gov.au/metric conversion.

"There is no doubt that a plant-based, whole-foods centered diet is the healthiest way to eat. The evidence is overwhelming."

"Smell the flowers, return the smiles and play with children." UNKNOWN